The Practical Stylist

Sheridan Baker

UNIVERSITY OF MICHIGAN

Thomas Y. Crowell Company   NEW YORK

ESTABLISHED 1834

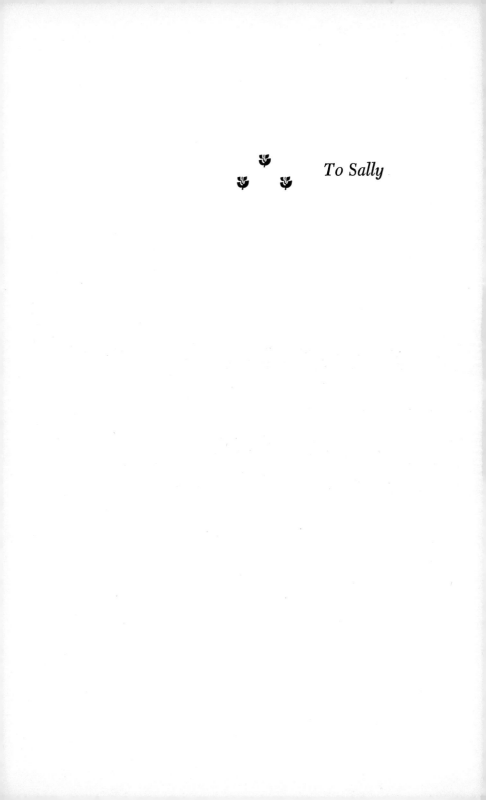

To Sally

Preface

THIS IS A RHETORIC primarily for freshman English, but I hope that it will also prove useful to the advanced student and to anyone who must face a blank page and the problems of exposition. From the first freshman essay through the last senior paper (and on through the doctoral dissertation and the company's annual report), the expository problems are always the same. Indeed, they all come down to two fundamental questions. The first is one of form; the second, one of style. And even form is a spatial styling. Since, in general, writing well is writing in style, I have found it practical to teach writing almost as a tactile art, in which the student learns how to shape his material and bring out the grain to best advantage. Hence *The Practical Stylist.*

I mean the book also to be practical in its brevity. Most freshman handbooks seem too big, too wordy, too involved. They seem to get mired in their own diligence and to stay stuck on the student's shelf. This book aims to travel light, to cover the ground without inordinate deliberation. I have included only what seems useful and essential. I think teachers will miss nothing that a more compendious handbook might contain.

To be sure, I omit some of the pedagogical favorites, such as definition and syllogistic reasoning, because I believe them secondary to more basic processes, which in fact manage most of the refinements without worrying about them. I emphasize argument, because I believe that argument subsumes all other expository principles, and that it teaches clearly and easily the firmest organization. So I begin with the argumentative thesis and include only a few exercises in simple exposition.

Many handbooks begin with simple units and build upward. I have found the opposite approach far more efficient. Once the student can push his material into a single argumentative thesis and can grasp the large essentials of structural arrangement, he can proceed easily to the smaller and smaller elements, which get the more powerful as they decrease in size—to paragraphs, to sentences and their punctuation, and on to the heart of the matter, to words, where the real dynamite, the real color and music is.

I have included exercises—in thesis-making, in paragraphing, in writing various kinds of sentences and punctuating them, in using words and spelling them, in handling various figures of speech. I have tried to encourage the student to play with language, to write unusual and complicated sentences for exercise, to juggle with words, much as the new courses in elementary mathematics start with numerical games and puzzles. For ballast, the study of words concludes with a chapter on usage and a short lexicon of practical prescriptions for good writing.

At this point the student should be ready for "Three Excursions," a chapter intended to sharpen his sense of language by exercises in how to put his personal experience directly into words, in how *not* to write, and in how to write irony. The book concludes with a chapter on the research paper, bringing the student's expository skills fully to bear. Inside the front cover is a list against which the student may check his work; inside the back cover, a set of symbols for marking errors. The book assumes a course of weekly essays arising from the usual freshman anthology, with no outside documentation necessary until the research paper.

The teacher will find plenty of room for his own course. He will undoubtedly find opportunity for that almost necessary bonus of academic gratification, disagreeing with the book—out of which much of our best teaching comes. He will certainly find a great deal that is familiar. Nothing here is really new. I am simply describing the natural linguistic facts discovered again and again by the heirs of Aristotle, in which lineage I seem inescapably to belong. For I have found that the one practical need in all writing is to mediate gracefully between opposite possibilities, between simplicity and complexity, clarity and shade, economy and plenitude, the particular and the general. I hope this book will help student and teacher to shoot the wickets pleasantly and well.

S. B.

Ann Arbor, Michigan
November, 1961

Acknowledgments

I HAVE ACQUIRED a number of devices from books and colleagues I can no longer trace, but I should like to acknowledge the general debt. Several particular debts I can declare. From Mark Schorer I learned the effectiveness of starting the class with the *thesis* and then working down. I am indebted to Robert C. Waddell's *Grammar and Style* (New York, 1951) for the idea behind my "Terrible Essay"; to Paul Roberts's *Understanding English* (New York, 1958) for the idea of exercises in the Latin and Greek prefixes; to Rudolf Flesch and the *Saturday Review* (January 14, 1961) for some suggestions about spelling; to Mr. Ullman Kilgore of Ann Arbor for a way to cure a split infinitive with an adjective; and to Mrs. Campbell Bonner, also of Ann Arbor, for thoughts on the predicate adjective and "I feel goodly."

I have adapted parts of two articles of mine: "Scholarly Style, or the Lack Thereof," *AAUP Bulletin*, XLII (1956), and "The Reason . . . Is Because," *College English*, XXI (1959). And I have borrowed a few sentences and phrases from among my contributions to *Style Manual for Biological Journals* (1960). I am especially grateful to Mr. Novello Grano of the Thomas Y. Crowell Company, without whose sense of style and excellent criticism this book would be much the poorer, and without whose initial suggestion it would probably not have been written at all.

Contents

5 / Punctuation 47

9 / The Research Paper 114

SAMPLE PAGES FROM A RESEARCH PAPER

1 / Thesis

The Stylistic Approach

STYLE IN WRITING is something like style in a car, a woman, or a Greek temple—a kind of linear mastery of materials that stands out from the landscape and compels a second look. It is some unique and unobtrusive synthesis of matter available to everyone; and, if a writer's style is really good, it will hang in the reader's memory and continue to bring wonder to the mind. Style is the product of a craftsman alive to experience and to the possibilities and the obstinacies in the material he works. It is a labor of love, and like love it can bring pleasure and satisfaction. A writer should like words the way some people like stones. He should like phrasing and syntax, and the very punctuation that keeps them straight. His interest in language should equal his interest in what he has to say, or he will never get the two together in any way he can call his own. He will never convince or delight, or get a second look.

This is not to say that style is only for the gifted. Quite the contrary. There *is* a certain mystery about writing, just as there is about life. But the stylistic side of writing is, in fact, the only side that can be analyzed and learned. The stylistic approach is the most practical approach: you learn some specific things to do and not to do, as you would learn strokes in tennis. What your ultimate game is like is up to you, but you can at least begin in good form. Naturally, it takes practice. You have to keep at it. Like the doctor and the lawyer and the golfer and the tennis player, you just keep practicing—even to write a practically perfect letter. But if you like the game you can probably learn to play it well. You will at least be able to write a respectable sentence, and to express your thoughts clearly, without excessive puffing and flailing.

In the essay as in business, trying to get started and getting off on the wrong foot account for most of our lost motion. So you will start by learning how to find a thesis that will, in a sense, virtually organize your essay for you. Next you will study the relatively simple principles behind the structure of your essay and the structure of your paragraphs—the architecture of spatial styling. Then, for exercise, you will experiment with various styles of sentence, playing with length and complexity. And finally you will get down to words themselves. Here is where writing tells; and here, as in ancient times, you will be in touch with the mystery. But again, there are things to do and things not to do, and these can be learned. So, to begin.

WHERE ESSAYS FAIL

You can usually blame a bad essay on a bad beginning. If your essay falls apart, it probably has no primary idea to hold it together. "What's the big idea?" we used to ask. The phrase will serve as a reminder that you must find the "big idea" behind your several smaller thoughts and musings before you start to write. In the beginning was the *logos,* says the Bible—the idea, the plan, caught in a flash as if in a single word. Find your *logos,* and you are ready to round out your essay and set it spinning.

The central idea, or thesis, is your essay's life and spirit. If your thesis is sufficiently firm and clear, it may tell you immediately how to organize your supporting material and so obviate elaborate planning. If you do not find a thesis, your essay will be a tour through the miscellaneous. An essay replete with scaffolds and catwalks—"We have just seen this; now let us turn to this"—is an essay in which the inhering idea is weak or nonexistent. A purely expository and descriptive essay, one simply about "Cats," for instance, will have to rely on outer scaffolding alone (some orderly progression from Persia to Siam) since it really has no idea at all. It is all subject, all cats, instead of being based on an idea *about* cats.

THE ARGUMENTATIVE EDGE

Find your thesis. The *about*-ness puts an argumentative edge on the subject. When you have something to say *about* cats, you have found your underlying idea. You have something to defend, something to fight about: not just "Cats," but "The cat is really man's best friend." Now the hackles on all dog men are rising, and you have an argument on your hands. You have something to prove; you have a thesis.

"What's the big idea, Mac?" Let the impudence in that time-honored demand remind you that the best thesis is a kind of affront to somebody, a fly in the facial ointment of all conventions. No one will be very much interested in listening to you deplete the thesis "The dog is man's best friend." Everybody knows that already. Even the dog-lovers will be uninterested, convinced that they know better than you. But the cat . . . .

So it is with any unpopular idea. The more unpopular the point of view and the stronger the push against convention, the stronger the thesis and the more energetic the essay. Compare the energy in "Democracy is good" with that in "Communism is good," for instance. The first is filled with platitudes, the second with plutonium. By the same token, if you can find the real energy in "Democracy is good," if you can get down through the sand to where the roots and water are, you will have a real essay, for the opposition against which you generate your energy is the heaviest in the world: boredom. Probably the most energetic thesis of all, the greatest inner organizer, is some tired old truth that you cause to jet with new life, making the old ground green again.

To find a thesis is to narrow and define your subject to a workable size. Under "Cats" you must deal with all felinity from the jungle up, carefully partitioning the eons and areas, the tigers and tabbies, the sizes and shapes. The minute you proclaim the cat the friend of man, you have pared away whole categories and chapters and need only think up the arguments sufficient to overwhelm the opposition, or at least to leave them scratching their ears and panting. So, put an argumentative edge on your subject —and you will have found your thesis.

Simple exposition, to be sure, has its uses. You may want to tell someone how to build a dog house, how to can asparagus, how to follow the outlines of relativity, or even how to write an essay. Performing a few exercises in simple exposition will no doubt sharpen your insight into the problems of finding orderly sequences, of considering how best to lead your readers through the hoops, of writing clearly and accurately. It will also illustrate how much finer and surer an argument is.

You will see that picking an argument immediately simplifies the problems so troublesome in straight exposition: the defining, the partitioning, the narrowing of the subject. Actually, you can put an argumentative edge on the flattest of expository subjects. "How to build a dog house" might become "Building a dog house is a thorough introduction to the building trades, including architecture and mechanical engineering." "Canning asparagus" might become "An asparagus patch is a course in economics." "Relativity" might become "Relativity is not the inscrutable mystery many suppose." You have simply assumed that you have a loyal Opposition consisting of the uninformed, the uninterested, and the scornful. You have given your subject its edge; you have limited and organized it at a single stroke. So pick an argument, and you will automatically be defining and narrowing your subject, and all the partitions you don't need will fold up. Instead of dealing with things, subjects, and pieces of subjects, you will be dealing with an idea and its consequences.

Sharpen your thesis. Come out with your subject pointed. Take a stand, make a judgment of value. Be reasonable, but don't be timid. It is helpful to think of your thesis, your main idea, as a debating question—"Resolved: Old age pensions must go"—taking out the "Resolved" when you actually write the subject down. But your resolution will be even stronger, your essay clearer and tighter, if you can sharpen your thesis one punctilio further—"Resolved: Old age pensions must go because————." Fill in that blank and your worries are practically over.

Try, for instance: "Old age pensions must go because they are making people irresponsible." I don't know at all if that is true, and neither will you until you write your way into it, considering probabilities and alternatives and objections, and especially the underlying assumptions. In fact, no one, no master sociologist or future historian, can tell absolutely if it is true, so multiplex are the causes in human affairs, so endless and tangled the consequences. The basic assumption—that irresponsibility is growing —may be entirely false. No one can tell absolutely. But by the same token, your guess may be as good as another's. At any rate, you are now ready to write. You have found your *logos*.

Now you can put your well-pointed thesis on a card on the wall in front of you to keep from drifting off target. But you will now want to dress it for the public, to burnish it and make it comely. Suppose you try:

> Old age pensions, perhaps more than anything else, are eroding our heritage of personal and familial responsibility.

Too — one-sided. Must give show that all others effect

But is this true? Perhaps you had better try something like:

> Despite their many advantages, old age pensions may actually be *less*. eroding our heritage of personal and familial responsibility.

This is really your thesis, and you can write that down on a scrap of paper too.

Believe in your thesis. You will have noticed how your original assertion has mellowed. And not because you have resorted to cheap tactics, though tactics may get a man to the same place, but rather because you have brought it under critical inspection. You have asked yourself what is true in it: what can (and cannot) be assumed true, what can (and cannot) be proved true. And you have asked where you yourself stand.

You should, indeed, look for a thesis you believe in, something you can even get enthusiastic about. It is probably useful to practice arguing on both sides of a question, as debaters do. There is no better way to break up old ground and find what you can and do believe, at least for the moment. But the argument without the belief will be hollow. You can hardly persuade anyone if you can't persuade yourself.

Conversely, you must test your belief with all the objections you can think of, just as you have already tested your first proposition about old age pensions. First, you have acknowledged the most evident objection—that the opposition's view must have some merit—by starting your final version with "Despite their many advantages . . . ." Second, you have gone a little deeper by seeing that in your bold previous version you had, with the words *are eroding,* begged the question of whether responsibility is in fact undergoing erosion; that is, you had silently assumed that responsibility *is* being eroded. This is one of the oldest fallacies and tricks of logic. To "beg the question," by error or intent, is to take for granted that which the opposition has not granted, to assume as already proved that which is yet to be proved. But you have saved yourself. You have changed *are eroding* to *may be eroding*. You have gone further and deleted the *perhaps more than anything else*. You have come closer to the truth.

Truth, for many, is something mystical and awesome; for others, something remote and impractical. And you may wonder if it is not astoundingly presumptuous to go around stating theses before you have studied your subject from all angles, made several house-to-house surveys, and read everything ever written. A natural uncertainty and feeling of ignorance, and a misunderstanding of what truth is, can well inhibit you from finding a thesis. But no one knows everything. No one would write anything if he waited until he did. To a great extent, the writing of a thing is the learning of it.

So, first, make yourself a desperate thesis and get into the arena. This is probably solution enough. If it becomes increasingly clear that your thesis is untrue, no matter how hard you push it, turn it around and use the other end. If your convictions have begun to falter with:

Despite their many advantages, old age pensions undermine responsibility . . . .

Try it the other way around, with something like:

Although old age pensions may offend the rugged individualist, they relieve much want and anxiety, and they dispel much familial resentment.

You will now have a beautiful command of all the objections to your new position. And you will have learned something about human fallibility and the nature of truth.

We *are* fallible. Furthermore, the truth about our most teasing and insistent questions usually lies somewhere beyond our fingertips. You may know, or guess, the truth; you may believe that such-and-such is so. But often you can never know it or prove it in any physical way. And neither can anyone else. You can only take it on faith—as much faith as your temperament allows.

Differences of opinion, it is said, make a horse race, and we often hear that one man's opinion is as good as another's. But the race rather quickly proves that one man's opinion was wrong. There is no proof at all, however, of the opinion that Man O' War is the greatest three-year-old of all time. "All time" is a long time. All the returns are not yet in. And much of the past is beyond reach. But even this opinion, though we can never know for certain, is either right or wrong. All we can do is to weigh the probabilities, and believe.

Persuade your reader.   Once you believe in your proposition, you will discover that proving it is really a venture in persuasion. You have made a thesis, an hypothesis really—an opinion as to what the truth seems to be from where you stand, with the information you have. Oddly enough, your proof has nothing to do with *making* that opinion right or wrong. If it is right, it is right; if wrong, wrong—with or without proof. Your thesis is not "more right" after you have backed it with proof: it is merely shown to have been right all the time. Whether you got it in a flash or in a year's careful analysis makes no difference. You knew it from the moment of your conviction; now the skeptical reader must believe it too. You must give him enough evidence to persuade him that what you say is probably true, finding arguments that will stand up in the marketplace and survive the public haggle. You must find public reasons for your private convictions.

Don't apologize.   "In my opinion," the beginner will write repeatedly, until he seems to be saying "It is only *my* opinion, after all, so it can't be worth much." He has failed to realize that his whole essay represents his opinion—as to what the truth of the matter is. Don't make your essay a letter to Diary, or to Mother, or to Teacher, a confidential report of what happened to you last night as you agonized upon a certain question. "*To me*, Robert Frost is a great poet"—this is really writing about yourself. You are only confessing private convictions. To find the "public reasons" often requires no more than a trick of grammar: a shift from "*To me*, Robert Frost is . . ." to "Robert Frost is . . . ," from "*I thought* the book was good" to "The book is good," from you and your room last night to your subject and what it *is*. The grammatical shift represents a whole change of viewpoint, a shift from self to subject. You become the man of reason, showing the reader around firmly, politely, and persuasively.

Once you have effaced yourself from your thesis, once you have erased *to me* and *in my opinion* and all such signs of amateur terror, you may later let yourself back into the essay for emphasis or graciousness: "Mr. Watson errs, I think, precisely at this point." You can thus ease your most tentative or violent assertions, and show that you are polite and sensible, reasonably sure of your position but aware of the possibility of error. Again: the man of reason. But it is better to omit the "I" altogether than to write a junior autobiography of your discoveries and doubts.

Now, with clear conscience, you are ready to write. Your single thesis sentence has magically conjured up your essay. All you need now is some form to put it in.

EXERCISE

Convert each of the following general subjects into a debating resolution ("Resolved: Cats make better pets than dogs"; "Resolved: Old age pensions must go"):

tropical fish	teen-agers
knitting	badminton
fraternities	stamps
budgets	shoes
apples	books

3 important points
1) All essays have beginning,
middle, and end.
2) List your points in ascending
interest - most persuasive point
at the end.
3) Don't ignore the
opposition by
referring to briefly or
point by point

9/16

2/ Structure

BEGINNING, MIDDLE, AND END

BUILD YOUR ESSAY in three parts. There really is no other way. As Aristotle long ago pointed out, works that spin their way along through time need a beginning, a middle, and an end to give them the stability of spatial things like paintings and statues. You need a clear beginning to give your essay character and direction, so the reader can tell where he is going and can look forward with expectation. Your beginning, of course, will set forth your thesis. You need a middle to amplify, and absorb, and fulfill. This will be the body of your argument. You need an end to let the reader know that he has arrived and where he has gotten. This will be your final paragraph, a summation and reassertion of your theme.

Give your essay the three-part *feel* of beginning, middle, and end. The mind likes this triple order. Three has always been a magic number. The woodcutter always has three sons, or three daughters; even the physical universe has three dimensions. Three has a basic psychological appeal as strong as a triangle or pyramid —especially with words and music, which the mind must pick up out of the air and assemble for itself into something like a spatial structure, a total impression. Many a freshman essay has no structure and leaves no impression. It is all chaotic middle. It has no beginning, it just begins; it has no end, it just stops, fagged out at two in the morning.

The beginning must feel like a beginning, not like an accident.

It should be a full paragraph that lets your reader gently into the subject and culminates with your thesis. The end, likewise, should be a full paragraph, one that drives the point home, pushes the implications wide, and brings the reader to rest, back on middle C, giving a sense of completion with the tonic. The next chapter describes these two kinds of paragraph more fully. The middle, however, being the bulk of your essay, needs further structural consideration now.

MIDDLE TACTICS

Arrange your points in order of increasing interest. Once your thesis has sounded the challenge, your reader's interest is probably at its highest pitch. He wants to see how you can prove so outrageous a thing, or to see what the arguments are for this thing he has always believed but never tested. Each step of the way into your demonstration he is learning more of what you have to say. But unfortunately his interest may be relaxing as it becomes satisfied: the reader's normal line of attention is a progressive decline, arching down like a wintry graph. Against this decline you must oppose your forces, so that the vector of your reader's interest will continue at least on the horizontal, with no sag, and preferably with an upward swing:

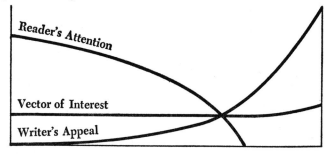

This is the basic principle for organizing the middle of your essay. Save your best till last. It is as simple as that.

Each successive item of your presentation should be more interesting than the last, or you will suddenly seem anticlimactic. Actually, minor regressions of interest make no great difference so long as the whole tendency is uphill and your last item clearly the best. Suppose, for example, you were to undertake the cat thesis. You decide that four points would make up the case, and that you might arrange them in the following order of increasing interest: (1) cats are affectionate but make few demands; (2) cats actually can look out for themselves; (3) cats have, in fact, proved extremely useful to man throughout history in controlling mice and other plaguy rodents; (4) cats satisfy some basic need in man for a touch of the jungle, savagery in repose, ferocity in silk, and have been worshipped for the exotic power they still seem to represent, even dozing on the banister. It may be, as you write, thinking things up, that you will find Number 1 developing attractive or amusing instances, and perhaps even virtually usurping the whole essay. Numbers 2, 3, and 4 should then be moved in ahead as interesting but brief preliminaries. Your middle structure, thus, should range from least important to most important, from simple to complex, from narrow to broad, from pleasant to hilarious, from mundane to metaphysical—whatever "leasts" and "mosts" your subject suggests.

Acknowledge and dispose of the opposition. Your cat essay, because it is moderately playful, can proceed rather directly, throwing only an occasional bone of concession to the dogs. But a serious controversial argument demands one organizational consideration beyond the simple structure of ascending interest. Although you have taken your stand firmly as a *pro*, you will have to allow scope to the *con*'s, or you will seem not to have thought much about your subject. The more opposition you can manage as you carry your point, the more triumphant you will seem, like a man on a high wire daring the impossible.

The basic organizing principle here is to get rid of the opposition first, and to end on your own side. Probably you will have already organized your thesis sentence in a perfect pattern for your *con-pro* argument:

Despite their many advantages, old age pensions . . . .
Although dogs are fine pets, cats . . . .

The subordinate clause states the subordinate part of your argument, which is your concession to the *con* viewpoint; your main clause states your main argument. As the subordinate clause comes first in your thesis sentence, so with the subordinate argument in your essay. Sentence and essay both reflect a natural psychological principle. You want, and the reader wants, to get the boys off the street so the men can have room. And you want to end on your best foot. (You might try putting the opposition last, just to see how peculiarly the last word insists on seeming best, and how, when stated last by you, the opposition's case seems to be your own.)

If the opposing arguments seem relatively slight and brief, you can get rid of them all together in one paragraph before you get down to your case. Immediately after your beginning, which has stated your thesis, you write a paragraph of concession: "Of course, security is a good thing. No one wants old people begging." And so on to the end of the paragraph, deflating every conceivable objection. Then back to the main line: "But the price in moral decay is too great." The structure might be diagrammed something like this:

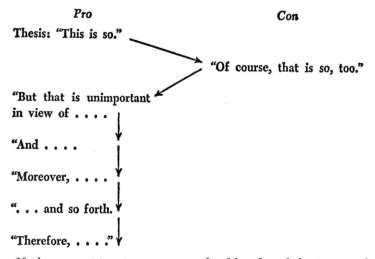

If the opposition is more considerable, demolish it point by point, using a series of *con*'s and *pro*'s. Each paragraph can be a small argument that presents the opposition, then knocks it flat—a kind of Punch and Judy show in series: "It must be admitted that . . . . But . . . ." And down goes the poor old opposition again. The structural line might look like this:

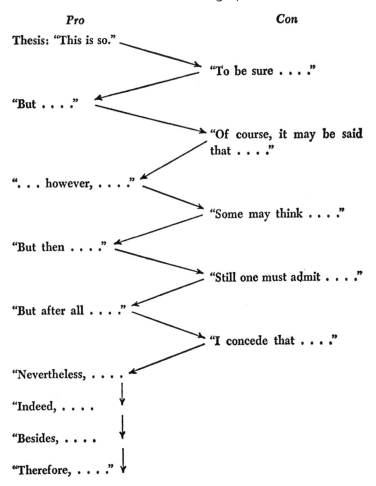

Pro   *Con*

Thesis: "This is so."

"To be sure . . . ."

"But . . . ."

"Of course, it may be said that . . . ."

". . . however, ..."

"Some may think . . . ."

"But then . . . ."

"Still one must admit . . . ."

"But after all . . . ."

"I concede that . . . ."

"Nevertheless, ...

"Indeed, ...

"Besides, ...

"Therefore, ..."

You will notice that *But* and *however* are always guides for the *pro's*, serving as switches back to the main line. You will do well to make yourself two lists of these switching words and phrases, one for the *pro's* and one for the *con's*, adding to those I have used above, to get the feel of the argumentative turn and to have them handy. *But, however,* and *Nevertheless* are the basic *pro's*. *But* always heads its turning sentence (not followed by a comma); *Nevertheless* usually does (followed by a comma). I am sure, however, that *however* is always better buried in the sentence between commas; *But* for the quick turn; the inlaid *however* for the more elegant sweep.

Run your comparisons point by point. Don't write all about sheep for three pages, then all about goats. Every time you say something about a sheep, say something comparable about a goat, pelt for pelt, horn for horn, beard for beard. Otherwise your essay will fall in two, and any sheep-points you want to develop among the goats will have to be repeated. The tendency to organize comparisons by halves is so strong that you will probably find you have fallen into it unawares, and in rewriting you will have to reorganize everything point for point—still arranging your pairs of points from least important to most. Finally, the only comparison worth making is one that aims to demonstrate a superiority, one, that is, with a thesis—"Resolved: Sheep are more useful than goats."

Now you have almost finished your essay. You have found a thesis. You have worked it into a decent beginning. You have then worked out a convincing middle, with your arguments presented in a sequence of ascending interest; you have used up all your points and said your say. You and your argument are both exhausted. But don't stop. You need an end, or the whole thing will unravel in your reader's mind. You need to buttonhole him in a final paragraph, to imply "I told you so" without saying it, to hint at the whole round experience he has just had, and to leave him convinced, satisfied, and admiring. One more paragraph will do it: beginning, middle, *and* end.

EXERCISES

1. Write five thesis sentences, each in three versions, the first version to be the simple debating resolution ("Resolved: Sheep are more useful than goats"), the second to add a *because* clause broad enough to cover a good case, the third to be the gentle version that might actually appear in your hypothetical essay.

2. Write five *con*-and-*pro* thesis sentences, beginning "Although . . . ."

3. Write a 500-word description of a process you know well—how to plan a vacation, how to play winning croquet, how an internal combustion engine works. This is straight exposition. It will introduce you to the fine dry air of objectivity; to the problem of laying out in orderly sequence, for the reader's gathering comprehension, details that are in fact

simultaneous; and to the difficulty of finding the clear, accurate, and descriptive phrase.

4. Now find a thesis that will change this description into an argument making some statement *about* the subject: the best-planned vacations can be disastrous; winning croquet is no child's play; what's under the hood is really no mystery. Rewrite the first paper using your new thesis and using, in some way, everything you said before.

5. Write a series of three-paragraph argumentative essays, conveying a thorough sense of beginning, middle, and end. (One of the best stylists I know, a German whose command of English is a living rebuke to American education, told me that his grasp of organization comes from having had to write, through a number of grammar-school years, nothing but three-paragraph essays. The treatment appears to have been excellent.)

6. Take a conventional proposition, like "Democracy is good" or "The dog is man's best friend," and write down as many unusual and interesting supporting arguments as you can think of, ones that would really stick. Arrange your items in order of increasing interest.

7. Write an outline of a comparative argument. State your thesis; then simply list your points in order of increasing interest, phrasing them in the general pattern of "Football is good, but baseball is better."

Beginning paragraph - funnel
Middle paragraph - consistent length (good for thinking) (check)

3 / Paragraphs

End paragraph - inverted funnel

THE STANDARD PARAGRAPH

A PARAGRAPH is a structural convenience. You build your essay with paragraphs, with blocks of concrete ideas, and they must fit smoothly. But they must also remain as perceptible parts, to rest your reader's eye and mind. Indeed, the paragraph originated, among the Greeks, as a resting place and place-finder, being first a mere mark (*graphos*) in the margin alongside (*para*) an unbroken sheet of handwriting—the proofreader's familiar ¶. A paragraph is a single idea, we hear; and this is true. But so is a word, usually; and so is a sentence, sometimes. It seems best, after all, to think of a paragraph as something you, as writer, use for the reader's convenience, rather than as some granitic form exuded by molten logic.

The medium determines the size of the paragraph. Your average longhand paragraph may look the same size to you as a typewritten one, and both may seem the same size as one in a book. But the printed page might show your handwritten paragraph so short as to be embarrassing, and your typewritten paragraph barely long enough for decency. Handwriting plus typewriting plus insecurity equals inadequate paragraphs. Your first impulse may be to write little paragraphs, often only a sentence to each. If so, you are not yet writing in any medium at all.

Of course, journalists are habitually one-sentence paragraphers —because the newspaper column makes a sentence look like a paragraph. The narrow columns and short paragraphs serve the rapid transit for which newspapers are designed. A paragraph from a book might fill a whole newspaper column with solid lead. It would have to be broken—paragraphed—for the reader's convenience. On the other hand, a news story on the page of a book would look like a gap-toothed comb, and would have to be consolidated for the reader's comfort.

Plan for the big paragraph. Imagine yourself writing for print —in a book, not a newspaper. Force yourself to four or five sentences at least, visualizing your paragraphs as about all of a size. Think of them as identical rectangular frames to be filled. This will allow you to build with orderly blocks, to strengthen your feel for structure. Since the beginner's problem is usually one of thinking of things to say rather than of trimming the overgrowth, you can do your filling-out a unit at a time, always thinking up one or two sentences more to fill the customary space. You will probably be repetitive and wordy at first—since this is our universal failing —but you will soon learn to fill your paragraph with clean and interesting details. You will develop a kind of constructional rhythm as you yourself come to a resting place at the end of your customary paragraphic frame. Once accustomed to a five-sentence frame, say, you can then begin to vary the length for structural and rhetorical emphasis, letting a good idea swell out beyond the norm, or bringing a particular point home in a paragraph short and sharp.

Find a topic sentence. Looked at as a convenient structural frame, the paragraph reveals a further advantage. It, like the essay itself, has a beginning, a middle, and an end. The beginning and the end are usually each one sentence long, and the middle gets you smoothly from one to the other. Since the paragraph, like the essay, flows through time, the last sentence is the most emphatic. This is your home punch. The first sentence holds the next most emphatic place. It will normally be your *topic sentence*, stating the small thesis of a miniature essay, something like this:

> *Jefferson believed in democracy because of his fearless belief in reason.* He knew that reason was far from perfect, but he also knew that it was the best we had. He knew that it was better than all the frightened and angry intolerances with which we fence off our own back yards at the cost of injustice. Thought must be free. Discussion must be free. Reason must be free to range among the widest possibilities. Even the opinion we hate, and have reasons for believing wrong, we must leave free so that

reason can operate on it, so that we advertise our belief in reason and demonstrate a faith unafraid of the consequences—because we know that the consequences will be right. Freedom is really not the aim and end of Jeffersonian democracy: freedom is the means by which democracy can rationally choose justice for all.

If your topic sentence covers everything within your paragraph, you are using your paragraphs with maximum effect, leading your reader into your community block by block. If your end sentences bring him briefly to rest, he will know where he is and appreciate it.

BEGINNING PARAGRAPHS: THE FUNNEL

State your thesis at the end of your beginning paragraph. Your beginning paragraph must contain your main idea, and present it to best advantage. Its topic sentence is also the *thesis sentence* of your entire essay. The clearest and most emphatic place for your thesis sentence is at the *end*—not at the beginning—of the beginning paragraph. If you put it first, you will have to repeat some version of it as you bring your beginning paragraph to a close; if you put it in the middle, the reader will very likely take something else as your main point—probably whatever the last sentence contains. The inevitable psychology of interest, as you move your reader through your first paragraph and into your essay, urges you to put your thesis last—in the last sentence of your beginning paragraph.

Think of your beginning paragraph, then, not as a frame to be filled, but as a funnel. Start wide and end narrow:

BROAD GENERALIZATION

THESIS

If you wished to show that Mozart's superiority lay in putting musical commonplaces to new uses, for instance, you would want to start at some small distance back from that point. You could start almost anywhere, but you should certainly start with some innocuous and peaceable proposition: "Mozart is one of the great names in music" or "Everyone likes the familiar" or "Music undoubtedly has charms for everyone." Your opening line, in other words, should be innocent, acceptable, and inoffensive, something to which all readers would agree without rise in blood pressure. (Antagonize and startle if you wish, but beware of losing your friends and of making your thesis an anticlimax.) Therefore: broad and genial. From the opening pleasant generalization you move progressively down to particulars. You narrow down: for example, from all music, to eighteenth-century music, to eighteenth-century musical commonplaces, to Handel and Mozart, to Mozart, to "the surprising turn and depth Mozart gives to the most conventional of musical phrases" (your thesis). Your paragraph might run, from broad to narrow, something like this:

> All people, even the tone-deaf, like some kind of music, and the old and familiar is usually the most appealing. For modern listeners, the eighteenth century usually represents this kind of comfortable familiarity—undemanding, pleasant, and commonplace. Indeed, eighteenth-century music developed and used a number of musical commonplaces. Composers were all working in the same style, tonality, and phraseology, and they often sound very much alike. Many people will say, for instance, that Handel and his musical heir, Mozart, are as like as two peas. But Mozart far outdid his master. He used Handel's conventions, but in those very conventions he found new expressive power. Indeed, Mozart's genius may be said to lie in his ability to use the commonplace but to make it continually surprising, fresh, and deep. We get the old with the ever surprisingly new.

Now, that paragraph turned out a little different from what I anticipated. I even found myself violating my rule of placing the thesis last. I went one sentence further for emphasis and for coherence with the first sentence. But it illustrates the funnel, from the broad and general to the one particular point, which is the main idea, the thesis. Here is another example:

Everyone likes a garden, even if for nothing more than a look in driving by. As man put down paving stones and discovered cement, he also discovered that he needed a little space for something green and growing. However much he may like the comfort of a house and the security of a city, he cannot completely cut himself off from nature. Even the tenement dweller will devise his window box. And suburbia represents a kind of mass movement into the lawns and shrubbery. But few of the onlookers ever realize how much work a garden can be.

MIDDLE PARAGRAPHS

Make your middle paragraphs full, and use transitions. The middle paragraph is the standard paragraph, the little essay in itself, with its own little beginning and little end. But it must also declare its allegiance to the paragraphs immediately before and after it. Each topic sentence must somehow hook onto the paragraph above it, must include some kind of transitional word or phrase. You may simply repeat a word from the sentence that ended the paragraph just above. You may bring down a thought left slightly hanging in air: "His ideas are different" might be a tremendously economical kind of topic sentence with automatic transition. Or you may get from one paragraph to the next by the usual stepping stones, like *but, however, nevertheless, therefore, indeed, of course.* One brief transitional touch in your topic sentence is usually sufficient.

The topic sentences in each of the following three paragraphs by Mr. W. H. Auden contain neat transitions. I have just used an old stand-by myself: repeating the words *topic sentence* from the close of the preceding paragraph. Mr. Auden, a distinguished poet, is explaining something about poetry and something about himself as he accepts the chair of Professor of Poetry at Oxford. He has been explaining how accidental and diverse a growing poet's background is. He now moves into the subject of formal education with a *then* making the transition from general diversity to academic diversity. In the next paragraph *But this* does the trick; in the last, *however.* The paragraphs are nearly the same length, all cogent, clear, and full. No one-sentence paragraphing here, no gaps, but all a lively, orderly progression:

It is hardly surprising, then, if a young poet seldom does well in his examinations. If he does, then either he is also a scholar in the making, or he is a very good boy indeed. A medical student knows that he must study anatomy in order to become a doctor, so he has a reason for study. A future scholar has a reason, because he knows more or less what he wants to know. But there is nothing a would-be poet knows he has to know. He is at the mercy of the immediate moment because he has no concrete reason for not yielding to its demands, and, for all he knows, surrendering to his immediate desire may turn out later to have been the best thing he could have done. His immediate desire can even be to attend a lecture. I remember one I attended, delivered by Professor Tolkien. I do not remember a single word he said, but at a certain point he recited, and magnificently, a long passage of *Beowulf*. I was spellbound. This poetry, I knew, was going to be my dish. I became willing, therefore, to work at Anglo-Saxon because, unless I did, I should never be able to read this poetry. I learned enough to read it, however sloppily, and Anglo-Saxon and Middle English poetry have been one of my strongest, most lasting influences.

But this was something which neither I nor anybody else could have foreseen. Again, what good angel lured me into Blackwell's one afternoon and, from such a wilderness of volumes, picked out for me the essays of William Paton Ker? No other critic whom I have subsequently read could have granted me the same vision of a kind of literary All Souls Night in which the dead, the living, and the unborn writers of every age and in every tongue were seen as engaged upon a common noble and civilizing task. No other could have so instantaneously aroused in me a fascination with prosody, which I have never lost.

You must not imagine, however, that being a bad boy is all fun. During my three years as an undergraduate, I had a high old time, I made some lifelong friends, and I was more unhappy than I have ever been before or since. I might or might not be wasting my time—only the future would show—I was certainly wasting my parents' money. Nor must you think that, because he fails to study, a young poet looks down his nose at all the scholarly investigations going on around him. Unless he is very young indeed, he knows that if it had not been for scholars working themselves blind copying and collating manuscripts, many poems would be unavailable, including those of Catullus, and many others full of lines that made no sense. Nor has the invention of printing made editors unnecessary. Lucky the poet whose collected works are not full of misprints.*

END PARAGRAPHS: THE INVERTED FUNNEL

Reassert your thesis. If the beginning paragraph is a funnel, the end paragraph is a funnel upside down: the thought starts moderately narrow—it is more or less the thesis you have had all the time—and then pours out broader and broader implications and finer emphases. The end paragraph reiterates, summarizes, and emphasizes with decorous fervor. This is your last chance. This is what your reader will carry away—and if you can carry *him* away, so much the better. All within decent intellectual bounds, of course. You are the man of reason still, but the man of reason surcharged with conviction, sure of his idea and sure of its importance.

The last paragraph conveys a sense of assurance and of repose, of business completed. Your topic sentence should be some version of your original thesis sentence, since the end paragraph is the exact structural opposite and complement of the beginning one. Its transitional word or phrase is often one of finality or summary —*then, finally, thus,* and *so:*

Mozart's commonplaces, then, are like proverbs—old truths in surprisingly new situations.

And so the beautiful garden grew more problems than roses.

The paragraph would then proceed to expand and elaborate this revived thesis. We would get an earnest epitome of Mozart's particular beauty, and of his ultimate quality and value; we would get an amusing sense of the gardener's endless buying of spray and fertilizer, his despair in trying to sweep back the waves of weeds. One rule of thumb: the longer the paper, the more specific the summary of the points you have made. A short paper will need no specific summary of your points at all; the renewed thesis and its widening of implications are sufficient.

Here is an end paragraph of Sir James Jeans's. His transitional word is *Thus.* His thesis was that the sky is blue because the short blue light-waves are diffused by dust and the long red ones are not:

* "Making and Judging Poetry," *Atlantic Monthly,* January, 1957, pp. 46–47.

Thus the different constituents of sunlight are treated in different ways as they struggle through the earth's atmosphere. A wave of blue light may be scattered by a dust particle, and turned out of its course. After a time a second dust particle again turns it out of its course, and so on, until finally it enters our eyes by a path as zigzag as that of a flash of lightning. Consequently the blue waves of the sunlight enter our eyes from all directions. And that is why the sky looks blue.

Here is the end paragraph of Auden's Oxford address. His transitional word is *Whatever*, since he has been talking about the different kinds of poems that can express a poet's "sacred encounters of his imagination." His thesis was that there is something both unexpected and mysterious about a poet's arrival at a poem:

> Whatever its actual content and overt interest, every poem is rooted in imaginative awe. Poetry can do a hundred and one things, delight, sadden, disturb, amuse, instruct—it may express every possible shade of emotion, and describe every conceivable kind of event, but there is only one thing that all poetry must do: it must praise all it can for being and for happening.*

Here is an end paragraph of Professor Richard Hofstadter's. His transitional word is *intellectuals*, carried over from the preceding paragraph. His thesis was that intellectuals should not abandon their defense of intellectual and spiritual freedom, as they have tended to do, under pressure to conform:

> This world will never be governed by intellectuals—it may rest assured. But *we* must be assured, too, that intellectuals will not be altogether governed by this world, that they maintain their piety, their longstanding allegiance to the world of spiritual values to which they should belong. Otherwise there will be no intellectuals, at least not above ground. And societies in which the intellectuals have been driven underground, as we have had occasion to see in our own time, are societies in which even the anti-intellectuals are unhappy.

* Auden, p. 52.

E X E R C I S E S

1. Write three beginning paragraphs, five or six sentences each, working down in each to some terse thesis such as one of these: "Without health there is nothing." "Reason is best." "Everything is relative." "Always prepare for the worst." "Live for the day." "Worry is good."

2. Write ten topic sentences for end paragraphs, each with a different transitional tag, as in these examples: "Ill health, *then*, darkens every prospect and discolors every thought." "It is clear, *therefore*, that ill health has produced more truth and more beauty—more art, more literature, more music, and a good share of philosophy, history, invention, and scientific insight—than have all the muscles in all outdoors." "One can, *in the last analysis*, live only the present moment."

3. Write three unrelated middle paragraphs, about 200 words each. Make the topic sentences cover the contents, and give each topic sentence some transitional touch: "Fly fishing *is different*." "*But* Judaism acknowledges man as a social being." "F.D.R. *also* had his blind side."

4. Write an essay with uniform paragraphs, each one about 125 words long, each, after a good beginning paragraph with a thesis, having a good sharp topic sentence—and don't forget the end.

Passive voice: Not as direct. Unclear - sometimes Wordy

4 / Sentences

★ Important chapter.

ALL THIS TIME you have been writing sentences, as naturally as breathing—and perhaps with as little variation. Now for a close look at the varieties of the sentence. Some can be shaggy and tangled indeed. But they are all offshoots of the simple active sentence, the basic English genus *John hit Joe,* with action moving straight from subject through verb to object.

This subject-verb-object sentence can be infinitely grafted and contorted, but there are really only two general varieties of it: (1) the "loose, or strung-along," in Aristotle's phrase, and (2) the periodic. English naturally runs "loose"; our thoughts are by nature strung along from subject through verb to object, with whatever comes to mind simply added as it comes—a trait happily acquired from French as a result of the Norman Conquest. But we can also use the periodic sentence characteristic of our German and Latin ancestry, in which ideas hang in the air like girders until all interconnections are locked by the final word: *John, the best student in the class, the tallest and most handsome, hit Joe.*

So we have two varieties of the English sentence, partly because its old Germanic oak was first limbered by French and then cured by Latin, but mostly because (as Aristotle observed of Greek) the piece-by-piece and the periodic species simply represent two ways of thought: the first, the natural stringing of thoughts as they come; the second, the more careful contrivance of emphasis and suspense.

THE SIMPLE SENTENCE

Use the simple active sentence, loosely periodic. Your best sentences will be hybrids of the loose and the periodic. First, learn to use active verbs (*John* HIT *Joe*), which will keep you within the simple active pattern with all parts showing (subject-verb-object), as opposed to verbs in the passive voice (*Joe* WAS HIT *by John*), which throw your sentences into the shade. Then learn to give your native strung-along sentence a touch of periodicity and suspense.

Any change in normal order can give you unusual emphasis, as when you move the object ahead of the subject:

That I like.
The house itself she hated, but the yard was grand.
Nature I loved; and next to Nature, Art.
Red suspenders, of all things, he chose.

You can vary the subject-verb-object pattern more gently by interruptive words and phrases, so that the meaning gathers excitement from the delay. The *of all things* does more for the red suspenders than the words themselves could manage: the phrase postpones the already postponed subject and predicate. Put the phrase last, and the emphasis fades considerably; the speaker grows a little sad, incredulous, resigned: "Red suspenders he chose, of all things." Put the sentence in normal order—"He chose red suspenders, of all things"—and we are, in fact, back to normal.

We expect our ideas one at a time, in normal succession—*John hit Joe*—and with anything further added, in proper sequence, at the end—*a real haymaker.* Change this fixed way of thinking, and you immediately put your reader on the alert for something unusual. Consequently, some of your best sentences will be simple active ones sprung wide with phrases coloring subject, verb, object, or all three, in various ways. You may, for instance, effectively complicate the subject:

A long black car, with two expressionless men in front, nobody in back, and muddy license plates conspicuous against its emphatic gloss, rolled softly by.

To come all this way, to arrive after dark, and then to find the place locked and black as ink made life almost unbearable.

Or the verb:

> He proceeded, carefully at first, then confidently, then with reckless steps, across the pasture.
>
> A good speech usually begins quietly, proceeds sensibly, gathers momentum, and finally moves even the most indifferent audience.

Or the object:

> She finally wrote the paper, a long desperate perambulation without beginning or end, without any guiding idea—without, in fact, much of an idea at all.
>
> His ruminations included the turtle in his back yard, the flowers and weeds, the great elm by the drive, the road, the earth, the stars, and the men and women of the village.

These are some of the infinite possibilities in the simple active sentence as it delays and attenuates and heightens the ordinary expectations of subject-verb-object.

Avoid the passive voice. The passive voice drones like nothing under the sun, bringing active English to a standstill. Of course, it can, in a string of active sentences, give mere variety, although phrasal and clausal variations are better. It can also vary the emphasis; it too depends on inverting normal order. *Joe was hit by John* throws selective light on Joe, by inverting regular consequences and distinguishing him from all other unfortunates, and it gives John a certain dubious distinction too. The passive voice can also, if need be, eliminate the doer altogether: *Joe was hit.* ("I was sunk." "It was done.")

In fact, your meaning sometimes demands the passive voice; the agent may be better under cover—insignificant, or unknown, or mysterious. The active "Shrapnel hit him" seems to belie the uncanny impersonality of "He was hit by shrapnel." Moreover, you may sometimes need the passive voice to place your true subject, the hero of the piece, where you can modify him conveniently: *Joe was hit by John, who, in spite of all . . . .* And sometimes it simply is more convenient: "This subject-verb-object sentence can be infinitely contorted." You can, of course, find a number of passive constructions in this book, which preaches against them, because they can also space out a thought that comes too fast and thick. A few paragraphs back, for instance, I changed "until all interconnections lock in the final word" (active) to ". . . are locked by the final word" (passive). The *lock* seemed too tight, especially with *in*, and the locking seemed contrary to the way buildings *are built.* Yes, the passive has its uses.

But avoid it if you can. It is wordy and unclear. It liquidates and buries the active individual. Our massed and scientific society is so addicted to the passive voice that the individual writer must constantly alert himself against its drowsy, soporific pomp. The simple English sentence is active; it *moves* from subject through verb to object: "Smith laid the cornerstone on April 1." But because we must sound important, because the impersonal institution must be bigger than Smith, the historian writes "The cornerstone was laid on April 1," and Smith vanishes from the earth. The doer and the writer both—all traces of individuality, all human interest—disappear behind the elongated passive verb: *was laid* instead of *laid.* Committees always write this way, and the effect on academic writing, as the professor goes from committee to desk to classroom, is astounding. "It was moved that a meeting would be held," the secretary writes, to avoid pinning the rap on anybody. So writes the professor, so writes the student.

The passive voice puts excess words in a sentence. Its dullness derives as much from its extra wordage as from its impersonality. *Joe was hit by John* says no more than *John hit Joe,* but takes forty per cent more words. The passive's inevitable *was* and *by* do nothing but connect; worse, all the *was's* and *by's* and *has been's* actually get in the way of the words carrying the meaning, like underbrush slowing you down and hiding what you want to see.

The best way to prune is with the active voice, cutting the passive and its fungus as you go. Notice the effect on the following typical, and actual, samples:

> Public concern *has* also *been given* a tremendous impetus *by* the findings of the Hoover Commission on the federal government, and "little Hoover" commissions to survey the organizational structure and functions of many state governments *have been established.* [In the federal government, the findings of the Hoover Commission *have* also greatly stimulated public concern, and many states *have established* "little Hoover" commissions to survey their governments. *28 words for 38*]

The algal mats *are made up of* the interwoven filaments of several genera. [The interwoven filaments of several genera *make up* the algal mats. *11 words for 13*]

Many of the remedies *would* probably *be shown to be* faith cures. [Many of the remedies *are* probably faith cures. *8 words for 12*]

Anxiety and emotional conflict *are lessened* when latency sets in. The total personality *is oriented* in a repressive, inhibitory fashion so as to maintain the barriers, and what Freud has called "psychic dams," against psychosexual impulses. [When latency sets in, anxiety and emotional conflict *subside*. The personality *inhibits* itself, maintaining its barriers—Freud's "psychic dams"—against psychosexual impulses. *22 words for 36*]

The passive voice, simply in its wordiness, is likely to be unclear even on the surface; but, if it eliminates the real subject of the verb, as it usually does, it is intrinsically unclear as well. "This passage has been selected because . . . ," the student will write, and the reader cannot tell who did the selecting. Does he mean that he, the writer, has picked it, or does he describe some process of natural or popular selection? We know he means himself, of course; but why doesn't he say so, and save a word, and avoid confusion? "I selected this passage because . . . ."

Any form of the verb *to be* may mean a passive construction. Our language must use some form of *to be* so frequently in stating that things *are* and in forming its compound verbs (*is falling, were playing*) that you should drop as many *is*'s and *was*'s as possible, simply to avoid monotony. But when they are—as they often are—signs of the passive voice, you can also avoid rigor mortis. And you can keep your sentences awake by not putting them in that favorite stretcher *there is . . . which* (or *there are . . . who* or *it is . . . that*): "Moreover, *there is* one class of worker *which* never seeks regular employment." The italicized words can disappear without a ripple.

Compound and Complex Sentences

Learn the difference between compound and complex sentences. You make a compound sentence by linking together simple sentences with coordinating conjunctions like *and, but, or,* or with a colon or a semicolon; you make a complex one by hooking lesser sentences onto the main sentence with *that, which, who,* or one of the many other subordinating connectives like *although, because, where, when, after, if.* The compound sentence *coordinates,* treating everything on the same level; the complex *subordinates,* putting everything else somewhere below its one main self-sufficient idea. The compound links ideas one after the other, as in the basic simple sentence; the complex is a simple sentence delayed and elaborated by clauses instead of merely by phrases. The compound represents the strung-along way of thinking; and the complex, the periodic.

Avoid simple-minded compounds. Essentially the compound sentence *is* simple-minded, a set of clauses on a string—a child's description of a birthday party, for instance: "We got paper hats and we pinned the tail on the donkey and we had chocolate ice cream and Randy sat on a piece of cake and I won third prize." *And . . . and . . . and.*

But this way of thinking is necessary, even in postgraduate regions. It is forever useful simply to pace off related thoughts, and to break the staccato of simple statement. And it often briskly connects cause and effect: "The clock struck one, and down he run." "The solipsist relates all knowledge to his own being, and the demonstrable commonwealth of human nature dissolves before his dogged timidity." The *and* can link clauses with all sorts of paces and effects, can bring in the next clause as a happy after-thought or a momentous consequence; and since the compound sentence is built on the most enduring of colloquial patterns—the simple sequence of things said as they occur to the mind—it has the pace, the immediacy, and the dramatic effect of talk. Hemingway, for instance, often gets all the numb hypertension of a shell-shocked mind by reducing his character's thoughts all to one level, in sentences something like this: "It was a good night and I sat at a table and . . . and . . . and . . . ."

With *but* and *or,* the compound sentence becomes more thoughtful. The mind is at work, turning its thought first one way then another, meeting the reader's objections by stating them. With semicolon and colon (or, if the clauses are very short, with comma), the compound grows more sophisticated still:

Men demand the most from themselves; women demand.
I came, I saw, I conquered.
Economic theorists assume a common man: he commonly wants
more than he can supply.

Think of the compound sentence in terms of its conjunctions—
the words that yoke its clauses—and of the accompanying punctuation.

GROUP I. *The three common coordinating conjunctions:*
and, but, *and* or (nor). *Put a comma before each.*

I like her, and I don't mind saying so.
Art is long, but life is short.

GROUP II. *Conjunctive adverbs:* therefore, moreover,
however, nevertheless, consequently, furthermore. *Put a semicolon
before, a comma after, each.*

Nations indeed seem to have a kind of biological span like the
ages of man himself, from rebellious youth, through caution, to
decay; *however,* this process is by no means inevitable.

GROUP III. *Some in-betweeners, which sometimes take
a comma, sometimes a semicolon, depending on your pace and
emphasis:* yet, still, so.

We long for the good old days, yet we never include the disadvantages.
Man longs for the good old days; yet he rarely takes into account
the inaccuracy of human memory and desire.
The preparation had been halfhearted and hasty, so the meeting
was wretched.
Rome declined into the pleasures of its circuses and couches; so
the tough barbarians conquered.

Learn to subordinate. You probably write compound sentences
almost without thinking; the subordinations of the complex usually
require some thought. You must pick your most important idea.
You must change the thoughtless *coordination* of mere sequence

into various forms of *sub*ordination. The birthday sentence, then, might come out something like this:

> After paper hats and chocolate ice cream and Randy sitting on a piece of cake and everyone pinning the tail on the donkey, I WON FIRST PRIZE.

You do the trick with connectives—with any word, like *after* in the sentence above, indicating time, place, cause, or other qualification:

> *If* he tries, *if* he fails, HE IS STILL GREAT *because* he is unbeaten.

You daily achieve subtler levels of subordination with the three relative pronouns *that, which, who,* and with the conjunction *that.* These connect thoughts so integral as to seem almost equal, but actually each tucks a clause (subject-and-verb) into some larger idea:

> The car, *which* runs perfectly, is not worth selling.
> The car *that* runs perfectly is worth keeping.
> He thought *that* the car would run forever.
> He thought [*that* omitted but understood] the car would run forever.

But the subordinating conjunctions and adverbs (words and phrases such as *although, if, because, since, until, where, when, as if, so that*) really put subordinates in their places. Look at *when* in this sentence of E. B. White's:

> Next morning *when* the first light came into the sky and the sparrows stirred in the trees, *when* the cows rattled their chains and the rooster crowed and the early automobiles went whispering along the road, Wilbur awoke and looked for Charlotte.

Here the simple *when,* used only twice, has regimented five subordinate clauses, all of equal rank, into their proper station below that of the main clause, "Wilbur awoke and looked for Charlotte." You can vary the ranking intricately and still keep it straight, if the mood should take you:

> *Although* some claim *that* time is an illusion, *because* we have no absolute chronometer, *although* the mind cannot effectively grasp time, *because* the mind itself is a kind of timeless presence almost oblivious to seconds and hours, *although* the time of our solar

system may be only an instant in the universe at large, WE STILL CANNOT QUITE DENY *that* some progression of universal time is passing over us, if only we could measure it.

Complex sentences are at their best really simple sentences gloriously delayed and elaborated. The following beautiful and elaborate sentence from the Book of Common Prayer is all built on the simple sentence "draw near":

Ye who do truly and earnestly repent you of your sins, and are in love and charity with your neighbors, and intend to lead a new life, following the commandments of God, and walking from henceforth in his holy ways, draw near with faith, and take this holy sacrament to your comfort, and make your humble confession to Almighty God, devoutly kneeling.

Even a short sentence may be complex, attaining a remarkably varied suspense. Notice how the simple statement "I allowed myself" is skillfully elaborated in this sentence by the late Wolcott Gibbs of *The New Yorker:*

Twice in my life, for reasons that escape me now, though I'm sure they were discreditable, I allowed myself to be persuaded that I ought to take a hand in turning out a musical comedy.

Once you glimpse the complexities possible within the outlines of the simple sentence, you are on your way to developing a prose capable of turns and glides, one with a kind of intellectual health that, no matter what the subject or mood, is always on its toes.

Try for still closer connections: modify. Your subordinating *if*'s and *when*'s have really been modifying—that is, limiting—the things you have attached them to. But there is a smoother way. It is an adjectival sort of thing, a shoulder-to-shoulder operation, a neat trick with no need for shouting, a stone to a stone with no need for mortar. You simply put clauses and phrases up against a noun, instead of attaching them with a subordinator. This sort of modification includes the following constructions, all using the same close masonry, though the degrees of subordination differ: (1) appositives, (2) relatives understood, (3) adjectives-with-phrase, (4) participles, (5) absolutes.

APPOSITIVES . Those phrases about shoulders and tricks and stones, above, are all in apposition with *sort of thing*, actually coordinate and interchangeable. They are stone-to-stone compressions of a series of sentences: "It is an adjectival sort of thing. It is a neat trick . . . ," and so forth. Mere contact does the work of the verb *is* and its subject *it*. English often does the same with subordinate clauses, omitting the *who is* or *which is* and putting the rest directly into apposition. "The William who is the Conqueror" becomes "William the Conqueror." "The Jack who is the heavy hitter" becomes "Jack the heavy hitter." These, incidentally, are called "restrictive" appositions, because they restrict to a particular designation the nouns they modify, setting this William and this Jack apart from all others (with no separating commas). Similarly, you can make nonrestrictive appositives from nonrestrictive clauses, those simply adding information (between commas). "Smith, who is a man to be reckoned with, . . ." becomes "Smith, a man to be reckoned with, ..." "Jones, who is our man in Liverpool, . . ." becomes "Jones, our man in Liverpool, ..." Restrictive or nonrestrictive, close contact makes your point. You glow with the pleasures of economy and fitness.

RELATIVES UNDERSTOOD . You can often achieve the same economy by omitting any kind of relative and its verb, thus gaining a compression both colloquial and classic:

A compression [that is] both colloquial and classic . . . .
The specimens [that] he had collected . . . .
The girl [whom] he [had] left behind . . . .

But be careful after verbs of feeling and seeing; omitting *that* may lead to confusion: "She felt his ears were too big." "He saw her nose was too small."

ADJECTIVES-WITH-PHRASE . Again making use of the appositive, adjectival idea, this construction is elegant, neat, and useful:

The law was passed, *thick with provisions and codicils, heavy with implications.*
There was the lake, *smooth in the early air.*

PARTICIPLES. Since participles are verbs acting as adjectives, they are extremely supple subordinators. Consider these three coordinate sentences:

He finally reached home. He discovered how tired he was. He went to bed without reading his mail.

By changing the main verbs into present participles, you can subordinate any two of the sentences to the other (so long as you still make sense), using the participles as adjectives to modify the subject *he:*

Finally *reaching* home, *discovering* how tired he was, he went to bed . . . .

The past participle has the same adjectival power:

Dead to the world, *wrapped* in sweet dreams, *untroubled* by bills, he slept till noon.

You will appreciate how like the adjective the participle is when you notice that *dead,* in the sentence above, is in fact an adjective, and that the participles operate exactly as it does.

Beware of dangling participles. They may trip you, as they have tripped others. The participle, with its adjectival urge, may grab the first noun that comes along, with shocking results:

Bowing to the crowd, the bull caught him unawares.
Observing quietly from the bank, the beavers disclosed several errors in judgment.
Squandering everything on beer, the money was never paid.
By bending low, the snipers could not see the retreating squad.
Tired and discouraged, half the lawn was still uncut.
What we need is a list of teachers broken down alphabetically.

Simply move the participle next to its intended noun or pronoun; you will have to supply this word if inadvertence or the passive voice has omitted it entirely. You may also save the day by changing a present participle to a past:

Observed quietly from the bank, the beavers . . . .
Squandered on beer, the money . . . .

Or you may move to ultimate sophistication by giving your participle a subject of its own within the phrase:

Every cent squandered on beer, the money was never paid.

Here is a sentence from Jane Austen's *Persuasion* that illustrates the adjectival and constructive power of the participle—*delighted* twice modifying *She* and subordinating everything to the one basic four-word clause that begins the sentence:

She always watched them as long as she could, delighted to fancy she understood what they might be talking of, as they walked along in happy independence, or equally delighted to see the Admiral's hearty shake of the hand when he encountered an old friend, and observe their eagerness of conversation when occasionally forming into a little knot of the navy, Mrs. Croft looking as intelligent and keen as any of the officers around her.

This sentence ends so gracefully because, with the phrase *Mrs. Croft looking,* it achieves the ultimate in participial perfection— the ablative absolute.

A B S O L U T E S . The absolute phrase has a great potential of polished economy. Many are simply prepositional phrases with the preposition dropped:

He ran up the stairs, [with] *a bouquet of roses under his arm,* **and rang the bell.**

He walked slowly, [with] *his gun at the ready.*

But the ablative absolute is the supreme sophisticate of subordination. If you have suffered the rudiments of Latin, you will probably remember it as a kind of awkward condensation something like *"The road completed,* Caesar moved his camp." But it survives in the best of circles. Somewhere E. B. White admits to feeling particularly good one morning, just having brought off an especially fine ablative absolute. The construction does have tone. And it is actually more common than you may suppose. A recent newspaper article stated that "the Prince has fled the country, *his hopes of a negotiated peace shattered."* The *hopes shattered* pattern (noun plus participle) marks the ablative absolute. The idea might have been more conventionally subordinated: "since his hopes were shattered" or "with his hopes shattered." But the ablative absolute accomplishes the subordination with economy and style.

Take a regular subordinate clause: "*When* the road *was* completed." Cut the subordinator and the finite verb. And you have an ablative absolute, a phrase that stands absolutely alone, shorn of both its connective *when* and its full predication *was*: "*The road completed,* Caesar moved his camp." Basically a noun and a participle, or noun and adjective, it is a kind of grammatical shorthand, a telegram: *ROAD COMPLETED CAESAR MOVED*—most said in fewest words, speed with high compression. This is its appeal and its power.

> The cat stopped, its *back arched,* its *eyes frantic* and *green.*
> The whole economy, *God willing,* soon will return to normal.
> *All things considered,* the plan would work.
> The *dishes washed,* the *baby bathed* and *asleep,* the last *ash tray emptied,* she could at last relax.

It is certainly a construction you should use with caution. It can sound exactly like a bad translation. But able writers come to it sooner or later, whether knowingly or through discovering for themselves the horsepower in a subordinate clause milled down to its absolute minimum of noun and participle, or noun and adjective, or even noun and noun. Hemingway uses it frequently. Here is one of the noun-noun variety at the end of a sentence about pistols in *To Have and Have Not:* ". . . their only *drawback the mess* they leave for relatives to clean up." And here are two noun-participle ones (*he playing* and *death administered*), in a passage that will serve as a closing illustration of how a complex sentence can subordinate as many as 164 words to the 7 of its one main clause ("they will put up with mediocre work"):

> If the spectators know the matador is capable of executing a complete, consecutive series of passes with the muleta in which there will be valor, art, understanding and, above all, beauty and great emotion, they will put up with mediocre work, cowardly work, disastrous work because they have the hope sooner or later of seeing the complete faena; the faena that takes a man out of himself and makes him feel immortal while it is proceeding, that gives him an ecstasy, that is, while momentary, as profound as any re-

ligious ecstasy; moving all the people in the ring together and increasing in emotional intensity as it proceeds, carrying the bullfighter with it, he playing on the crowd through the bull and being moved as it responds in a growing ecstasy of ordered, formal, passionate, increasing disregard for death that leaves you, when it is over, and the death administered to the animal that has made it possible, as empty, as changed, and as sad as any major emotion will leave you.*

PARALLEL CONSTRUCTION

Usid: So group together.

Use parallels wherever you can. Hemingway's 171-word sentence could not have held together without parallel construction, the masonry of syntax. No complex sentence can sustain a very long arch without it. Actually, Hemingway's "that is" after "ecstasy" makes a false parallel, throwing his arch briefly out of line (he should have used "which is" or something like "an ecstasy as profound, though momentary, as any . . ."). You have also seen examples of parallel ranking in White's *when* sentence (on page 32) and in the sentence that followed, dealing with time. The sentence about the cat and the one about the relaxing housewife (on page 37) have shown you ablative absolutes laid parallel.

Parallel masonry can be very simple. Any word will seek its own kind, noun to noun, adjective to adjective, infinitive to infinitive. The simplest series of things automatically runs parallel:

shoes and ships and sealing wax
I came, I saw, I conquered
to be or not to be
a dull, dark, and soundless day
mediocre work, cowardly work, disastrous work

But they very easily run out of parallel too, and this you must learn to prevent. The last item especially may slip out of line, as in this series: "friendly, kind, unobtrusive, and *a bore*" (boring). Thus your articles and prepositions should govern a series as a whole, or should accompany *every* item, or none:

a hat, a cane, a pair of gloves, and a mustache
a hat, cane, pair of gloves, and mustache

* *Death in the Afternoon* (New York: Scribner's, 1932), pp. 206–7.

by land, by sea, or by air
by land, sea, or air

Repeat your paralleling connectives. When your series consists of phrases or of clauses, you should repeat the preposition or conjunction introducing them, to ensure clarity:

> *By* weeks of careful planning, *by* intelligence, *by* thorough training, and *by* a great deal of luck . . . .
> *Since* all things are not equal, *since* consequences cannot be foreseen, *since* we live but a moment . . . .
> He looked *for* clean fingernails and polished shoes, *for* an air of composure, and *for* a quick wit.

Watch the paralleling of pairs. Pairs should be pairs, not odds and ends. Notice how the italicized portions of these sentences have been corrected:

> She liked *the lawn and gardening* (the lawn and the garden).
> They were all *athletic or big men on campus* (athletes or big men on campus).
> He wanted *peace without being disgraced* (peace without dishonor).
> He liked *to play well and winning before a crowd* (to play well and to win; playing well and winning).
> She was *shy but a nice girl* (shy but nice).

Check your terms on both sides of your coordinating conjunctions (*and, but, or*) and see that they match:

> **necessary**
> **Orientation week seems both worthwhile [adjective] and ~~a necessity~~** **[noun].**
>
> **that**
> **He prayed that they would leave and / the telephone would not ring.**

Learn to use paralleling coordinators. The first sentence above has used one of a number of useful (and tricky) parallel constructors: *both/and; either/or; not only/but also; not/but; first/second/third; as well as.* This last one is exactly like *and*, a simple link between two equivalents, but it often causes trouble:

A person should take care of his physical self [noun] *as well as* being [participle] able to read and write.

Again, the pair should be matched: "his physical self as well as his intellectual self," or "his physical self as well as his ability to read and write"—though this second is still slightly unbalanced, in rhetoric if not in grammar. The best cure would probably extend the underlying antithesis, the basic parallel:

A person should take care of his physical self as well as his intellectual self, of his ability to survive as well as to read and write.

With the *either-or*'s and the *not-only-but-also*'s you continue the principle of pairing. The *either* and the *not only* are merely signposts of what is coming: two equivalents linked by a coordinating conjunction (*or* or *but*). Beware of putting the signs in the wrong place—too soon for the turn.

(Either) he is an absolute piker or a fool.

(Neither) in time nor space . . . .

He (not only) likes the girl, but the family, too.

In these examples the thought got ahead of itself, as in talk. Just make sure that the word following each of the two coordinators is of the same kind, preposition for preposition, article for article, adjective for adjective—for even with signs well placed, the parallel can skid:

The students are not only organizing [present participle] social
                                   discussing
activities, but also ~~are-interested~~ [passive construction] ~~in~~ political questions.

Put identical parts in parallel places; fill in the blanks with the same parts of speech: "not only ———, but also ———." You do the same with numerical coordinators:

However variously he expressed himself, he unmistakably thought, first, *that* everyone could get ahead; second, *that* workers generally were paid more than they earned; and, third, *that* laws enforcing a minimum wage were positively undemocratic.

For a number of reasons he thought (1) that he did not like it,

(2) that she did not like it, (3) that they did not like it. [Note that the parentheses around the numbers operate exactly as any parenthesis, and need no additional punctuation.]

My objections are obvious: (1) it is unnecessary, (2) it costs too much, and (3) it won't work.

In parallels of this kind, *that* is usually the problem, since you may easily, and properly, omit it when there is only one clause and no confusion:

. . . he unmistakably thought everyone could get ahead.

If second and third clauses occur, as your thought moves along, you may have to go back and put up the first signpost:

that

. . . he unmistakably thought / everyone could get ahead, that workers . . . , and that laws . . . .

Enough of *that*. Remember simply that equivalent thoughts demand parallel constructions. Notice the clear and massive strategy in the following sentence from the concluding chapter of Freud's last book, *An Outline of Psychoanalysis*. Freud is summing up not only the previous discussion but the quintessence of his life's work. He is pulling everything together in a single sentence. Each of the parallel *which* clauses gathers up, in proper order, an entire chapter of his book (notice the parallel force in repeating *picture,* and the use of the dash):

The picture of an ego which mediates between the id and the external world, which takes over the instinctual demands of the former in order to bring them to satisfaction, which perceives things in the latter and uses them as memories, which, intent upon its self-preservation, is on guard against excessive claims from both directions, and which is governed in all its decisions by the injunctions of a modified pleasure principle—this picture actually applies to the ego only up to the end of the first period of childhood, till about the age of five.

Such precision is hard to match. This is what parallel thinking brings—balance and control and an eye for sentences that seem intellectual totalities, as if struck out all at once from the uncut rock. Francis Bacon also can seem like this (notice how he drops the verb after establishing his pattern):

For a crowd is not company, and faces are but a gallery of pictures, and talk but a tinkling cymbal, where there is no love.

Reading maketh a full man; conference a ready man; and writing an exact man.

And the balance can run from sentence to sentence through an entire passage, controlled not only by connectives repeated in parallel but by whole phrases and sentences so repeated, as in this passage by Macaulay:

> To sum up the whole: we should say that the aim of the Platonic philosophy was to exalt man into a god. The aim of the Baconian philosophy was to provide man with what he requires while he continues to be man. The aim of the Platonic philosophy was to raise us far above vulgar wants. The aim of the Baconian philosophy was to supply our vulgar wants. The former aim was noble; but the latter was attainable.

THE LONG AND SHORT OF IT

Your style will emerge once you can manage some length of sentence, some intricacy of subordination and parallel, and some play of long and short, of amplitude and brevity. Try the very long sentence, and the very short. The best short sentences are meatiest:

> To be awake is to be alive.
> A stitch in time saves nine.
> The mass of men lead lives of quiet desperation.
> The more selfish the man, the more anguished the failure.

Experiment, too, with the fragment, trying to cut and place it clearly (usually at beginnings and ends of paragraphs) so as not to lead your reader to expect a full sentence, or to suspect a poor writer:

> But no more.
> First, a look behind the scenes.
> Thoughts beyond words.
> Cabbages and kings.
> Enough of that.

The fragment is close to conversation. It is the laconic reply, the pointed afterthought, the quiet exclamation.

The conversational flow between long and short makes a passage move. Study the subordinations, the parallels, and the play of short and long in this elegant passage of Virginia Woolf's—after you have read it once for sheer enjoyment. She is writing of Lord Chesterfield's famous letters to Philip Stanhope, his illegitimate son:

But while we amuse ourselves with this brilliant nobleman and his views on life we are aware, and the letters owe much of their fascination to this consciousness, of a dumb yet substantial figure on the farther side of the page. Philip Stanhope is always there. It is true that he says nothing, but we feel his presence in Dresden, in Berlin, in Paris, opening the letters and poring over them and looking dolefully at the thick packets which have been accumulating year after year since he was a child of seven. He had grown into a rather serious, rather stout, rather short young man. He had a taste for foreign politics. A little serious reading was rather to his liking. And by every post the letters came—urbane, polished, brilliant, imploring and commanding him to learn to dance, to learn to carve, to consider the management of his legs, and to seduce a lady of fashion. He did his best. He worked very hard in the school of the Graces, but their service was too exacting. He sat down half-way up the steep stairs which lead to the glittering hall with all the mirrors. He could not do it. He failed in the House of Commons; he subsided into some small post in Ratisbon; he died untimely. He left it to his widow to break the news which he had lacked the heart or the courage to tell his father—that he had been married all these years to a lady of low birth, who had borne him children.

The Earl took the blow like a gentleman. His letter to his daughter-in-law is a model of urbanity. He began the education of his grandsons . . . .*

Those are some sentences to copy. We immediately feel the rhythmic play of periodic and loose, parallel and simple, long and short. Such orchestration takes years of practice, but you can always begin.

* The Second Common Reader, Harvest Books (New York: Harcourt, Brace, 1932), p. 81.

EXERCISES

1. Write a dozen short sentences that invert normal order for emphasis: "That I like."
2. Write a dozen simple sentences (make sure you have no subordinate clauses) that complicate (a) the subject, (b) the verb, and (c) the object.
3. Write a dozen sentences in the passive voice, and change each to its active equivalent.
4. Pick five obese and passive sentences from your textbooks (including this one, if the author has slipped). Change them to clean active sentences, indicating the number of words saved in each.
5. Write a dozen compound sentences, four with *and*, four with *but*, four with *or* (*nor*). Try to get as grand a feeling of consequence as possible: "Empires fall, and the saints come marching in."
6. Write a dozen compound sentences using conjunctive adverbs, on the pattern: "———; however, ———"—punctuated carefully with semicolon and comma.
7. List all the subordinators you can think of (*since, if, before,* etc.).
8. Write five sequences of three simple sentences on the pattern: "He finally reached home. He was tired. He went to bed." Then, changing verbs to participles, subordinate two of the sentences to the remaining one in each sequence.
9. To appreciate participial subordination, rewrite each of the following as a series of simple coordinate sentences, changing the participles into finite verbs and the principal adjectives into predicate adjectives ("They danced. They swayed . . . . Some were intense."):

They danced, swaying in dim light, dreaming happily, some laughing, some intense, some even embarrassed and awkward, wishing but failing to join the dream completely.

Fishing, hiking, playing cribbage, sometimes talking seriously, sometimes merely sitting together in silence, they spent the last of summer.

He was every inch a soldier, clipped, tailored, polished, as if straight from a musical comedy.

His train already late, his money stolen, his hat gone, his plans upset from start to finish, he hoped desperately that he still had time.

Complicated, misleading, inadequate, and motivated by special interests, the bill deserved defeat.

10. Write a dozen sentences with dangling participles, with a remedy for each.

11. Write a dozen sentences with ablative absolutes, six using present participles, six using past.

12. Now, write four 100-word sentences *with only one independent clause* in each, and with everything else subordinated.

13. Write ten sentences (two apiece) filling the blanks in each set of the following coordinators: both _____ and _____; either _____ or _____; not only _____ but also _____; (1) _____, (2) _____, and (3) _____; _____ as well as _____.

14. Adjust or clarify the parallels in the following (taken from freshman papers):

> These men are not only cheating themselves, but also are banded together into crime syndicates which help to lower the character of the entire nation.

> He stated two ways in which man could hope to continue survival. (1) World citizenship, or (2) destroying most of the inventions that man is uncertain of and go back to where we can understand ourselves and progress.

> In this way not only the teacher needs to be concerned with the poorest student, but every class member helped.

> A student follows not only a special course of training, but among his studies and social activities finds a liberal education.

> Education is something that can't be taken for granted but instead requires serious thought.

> When they go to church, it is only because they have to go and not of their own desire.

> Many people argue that the so-called virtues of man belong to the age of chivalry, and they do not apply to the present.

> This is not only the case with the young voters of the United States but also of the adult ones.

> . . . an education which will not only embarrass her but also is dangerous to a self-governing people.

> Certain things are not actually taught in the classroom. They are learning how to get along with others, to depend on oneself, and managing one's own affairs.

> Every time I sit down and attempt to read one of those interesting essays, or else studying German . . . .

> Knowing Greek and Roman antiquity is not just learning to

speak their language but also their culture.

I think fraternities are sociable as well as the dormitories.

All the girls now intend to get married as well as having families of three or four.

15. (a) In the following famous sentence of Bacon's, straighten the faulty parallels and fill out all the phrasing implied by them:

Histories make men wise; poets witty; the mathematics subtle; natural philosophy deep; moral grave; logic and rhetoric able to contend.

(b) Now write five sentences on the Baconian pattern: "Jack would eat no fat; his wife no lean; the old dog only soup . . . ; the young . . . ."

16. Write an imitation, or a parody, of the following passage from Samuel Johnson, matching him sentence for sentence and phrase for phrase ("Of genius, that power which constitutes a ball player . . . ." "Of glamour, that power which constitutes an actress . . . ."):

Of genius, that power which constitutes a poet; that quality without which judgement is cold and knowledge is inert; that energy which collects, combines, amplifies, and animates —the superiority must, with some hesitation, be allowed to Dryden. It is not to be inferred that of this poetical vigour Pope had only a little, because Dryden had more, for every other writer since Milton must give place to Pope; and even of Dryden it must be said that if he has brighter paragraphs, he has not better poems. Dryden's performances were always hasty, either excited by some external occasion, or extorted by domestick necessity; he composed without consideration, and published without correction. What his mind could supply at call, or gather in one excursion, was all that he sought, and all that he gave. The dilatory caution of Pope enabled him to condense his sentiments, to multiply his images, and to accumulate all that study might produce, or chance might supply. If the flights of Dryden therefore are higher, Pope continues longer on the wing. If of Dryden's fire the blaze is brighter, of Pope's the heat is more regular and constant. Dryden often surpasses expectation, and Pope never falls below it. Dryden is read with frequent astonishment, and Pope with perpetual delight.

17. Write an imitation of the passage from Virginia Woolf on page 43, aiming toward effective rhythms of short and long.

5 / Punctuation

Punctuation gives the silent page some of the breath of life. It marks the pauses and emphases with which a speaker points his meaning. Loose punctuators have forgotten what every good writer knows: that even silent reading produces an articulate murmur in our heads, that language springs from the breathing human voice, that the beauty and meaning of language depend initially on its auditory effects, its tuning of emphasis and pause. Commas and semicolons and periods do what they can to transcribe our meaningful pauses to the printed page.

THE PERIOD: SENTENCES AND FRAGMENTS

Learn what a sentence is. Having used sentences all our lives, we all think we know what one is. But commas still appear where periods should be, and the reader blunders ahead when he should have stopped. Think of a *sentence* as a subject completed in its verb, and tacked home with a period. A *phrase* presents no problem, since it has no verb. But a *clause,* which does have subject and verb, is nevertheless incomplete when it looks to the main sentence for fulfillment:

After the ball, the sweepers come. [Phrase]
After the ball is over, the sweepers come. [Clause]

Your sentence is complete if the first part clearly looks ahead toward the period, and if the end clearly looks back toward its beginning. If you find the first part of your sentence looking back, or looking ahead in vain, you have no sentence; you have a fragment that should be hooked, with a comma, where it belongs:

>**He dropped his teeth.** *Which had cost two hundred dollars.*
>**A good example is Hawthorne.** *A writer who can dramatize abstract moral theories.*
>**Cleopatra is the stronger.** *Trying to create Antony in her own Egyptian image.*

The accidental fragment is almost invariably found *after* the sentence to which it belongs.

But try an occasional rhetorical fragment. Nothing so firmly demonstrates your command over the sentence as the judicious use of an occasional fragment, as I have already suggested (p. 42). Make it stand alone, and no mistake. Fragments are safest and most effective, with all their transitional force, at the head of a paragraph. Such fragments are especially dramatic, economical, and close to speech:

>**First, a word to the wise.**
>**Another point.**
>**Of course.**
>**Not at all.**
>**Expert within limits, that is.**

Notice that all these fragments—condensations, afterthoughts, answers, quiet exclamations—usually omit some hypothetical form of *is,* with its subject:

>**First, [here is] a word to the wise.**
>**Of course, [it is *or* he did].**
>**[It is] not at all [so].**

This kind of dramatic fragment, in other words, is talking about existences, about what *is,* letting the words assert their own being. It is exactly the kind of streamlining the Latin writers liked, and it is still swift and racy. But be careful.

THE COMMA

Learn the rules. You need only four rules to use the comma expertly, and the last two employ the same principle. Use a comma:

I. Before *and, but, for, or, nor, yet, still,* when joining independent clauses.

II. Between all terms in a series, *including the last two.*

III. To set off parenthetical openers and afterthoughts.

IV. Before and after parenthetical insertions (use a *pair* of commas).

R U L E   I . *Use a comma before conjunctions such as* and, but, *and for, when joining independent clauses.*

You will be told that you may omit the comma when your two clauses are short: "He hunted and she fished." You certainly can get away with it, and in the best of publications. But it is really the first tiny slip toward utter abandon. Your clauses will grow longer. You will begin to touch in a comma only now and then, still leaving the main gap between clauses unplugged. You will omit commas before *but* and *for* and really throw your reader off. There is nothing wrong with "He hunted, and she fished." With the comma, in fact, it shows the slight pause that is there when you say it. Stick to the rule, and you can't go wrong. And you will greatly improve your sense of style.

Think of the ,and as a unit equivalent to the period. The period, the semicolon, and the ,and all separate independent clauses, but with different emphases:

  .   **He was tired. He went home.**
  ;   **He was tired; he went home.**
,and   **He was tired, and he went home.**

If you can only think of the ,and or the ,but as a unit, perfectly equivalent to the . and the ; as a buffer between independent clauses, you will have mastered the basic problem in punctuation, the cause of most trouble.

What you need is a firm rule to follow, one to break only in airier moments, with a full sense of release and a clear gain in meaning. Look again at White's *when* sentence:

Next morning when the first light came into the sky and the sparrows stirred in the trees, when the cows rattled their chains and the rooster crowed and the early automobiles went whispering along the road, Wilbur awoke . . . .

White omits several commas before *and,* but the reason is dazzlingly clear: he is regimenting short coordinate clauses under one subordinator, and a comma after *sky,* for instance, would block the *when* from the *sparrows* and throw the clauses out of rank. For reasons of rank, he also omits the "introductory" comma after *Next morning.* A comma here, since there are only two commas controlling the whole long sentence, would have made *Next morning* too prominent, making it seem equal to the long *when* elements.

Your punctuation, or lack of it, signals your meaning as it comes in, word by word. The **,and** tells your reader that a whole new predication is coming; just-plain-*and* tells him to expect only a smaller unit:

He hunted the hills and . . . .

brings an entirely different expectation from:

He hunted the hills, and . . . .

In the first you expect something like *dales,* something parallel to *hills.* In the second you expect another subject and predicate: "and he found . . . ," or "and they were . . . ."

Omitting the comma between independent clauses joined by *and* really makes a false parallel, and the silence of print has often encouraged our error. When you *say* "hills and dales," you do not pause. When you *say* ". . . hills, and he found . . . ," you do pause. English invariably expresses this difference in meaning by pausing or not. Modern linguists, who call this pause a "double-bar juncture," have reminded us that commas represent meaning.

The same may be seen with *but, or,* and *yet:*

She was naughty but nice.
She was naughty, but that is not our business.

Wear your jacket or coat.
Wear your jacket, or you will catch cold.

It was strong yet sweet.
It was strong, yet it was not unpleasant.

Of course, you may use a comma in *all* the examples above, if your sense demands it, because the contrast set by *but, or,* and *yet* often urges a comma, whether or not full predication follows: "It was strong, yet sweet." You will notice that you always pause where the commas are.

The comma before *for* and *still* is even more urgently needed. Without it, their conjunctive meaning changes; they assume their ordinary roles, *for* as a preposition, *still* as an adjective or adverb:

She liked him still . . . . [that is, either *yet* or *quiet!*]
She liked him, still she could not marry him.

She liked him for his money.
She liked him, for a good man is hard to find.

An observation: *for* is the weakest of all the coordinators—almost a subordinator, perilously close to *because*. *For* can seem moronic, if cause and effect are fairly obvious: "She liked him, for he was kind." Either make a point of the cause by full subordination—"She liked him *because* he was kind"—or flatter the reader with a semicolon: "She liked him; he was kind." *For* is effective only when the cause is somewhat hard to find: "Blessed are the meek, for they shall inherit the earth."

RULE II. *Use commas between all terms in a series, including the last two:*

words, phrases, or clauses in a series
to hunt, to fish, and to hike
He went home, he went upstairs, and he could remember nothing.
He liked oysters, soup, roast beef, wine, and women.

The linguists' recordings will show a pause between the last two items of a series as well as between any two: not *wine-and-women,* but *wine,* and *women.* The good punctuator would drop the last comma only if he meant *wine and women* as a unit equivalent to *oysters.* Since the last element will always have some climactic or anticlimactic effect, solemn or humorous, don't blur it into the one preceding. Keep *wine* and *women* separate.

By carefully separating all elements in a series, you keep alive a final distinction long since lost in the daily press, the one Mrs. Woolf makes (see p. 43): "urbane, polished, brilliant, imploring and commanding him . . . ." *Imploring and commanding* is syntactically equal to each one of the other modifiers in the series. If Mrs. Woolf customarily omitted the last comma, as she does not, she could not have reached for that double apposition. The muscle would have been dead. These other examples of double apposition can give you an idea of its effectiveness:

They cut out his idea, root and branch.
He lost all his holdings, houses and lands.
He loved to camp, to fish and to hunt.

A comma makes a great deal of difference, of sense and distinction. Notice the difference between the following adjectives in series:

a good, unexpected, natural rhyme
a good old battered hat

With adjectives in series only your sense can guide you. If each seems to modify the noun directly, as in the first example above, use commas. If each seems to modify the total accumulation of noun and adjectives, as with *good* and *old* in the second phrase, do not use commas. Say your phrases aloud, and put your commas in the pauses that distinguish your meaning.

One final, special case. You can sometimes join clauses without conjunctions (leaving only the comma):

She sighed, she cried, she almost died.
I couldn't do it, I tried, they all got away.
It passed, it triumphed, it was a good bill.
I came, I saw, I conquered.

The rhetorical intensity of this construction, which the Greeks called *asyndeton*, is obvious. The language is breathless, or grandly emphatic. As Aristotle once said, it is a person trying to say many things at once. The subjects repeat themselves, the verbs overlap, the idea accumulates a climax. By some psychological magic, the clauses of this construction usually come in groups of three. The comma is its sign. But unless you have a stylistic reason for such a flurry of clauses, go back to the normal conjunction, semicolon, or period.

RULE III. *Set off parenthetical openers and after-thoughts with a comma.*

Again, note the preliminary pause that expresses your meaning:

Besides, she hated it.
However, she liked him.
Inside, everything was snug.

For several reasons, they stayed home.
Being of stout heart, he dieted.
A fast man with a rocket, he still failed at bridge.

Although several looked bored, he kept on talking.
Because it never gets cold, they wear few clothes.
If it is not too much trouble, punctuate accurately.

First observation: A comma often makes all the difference:

However she tried, she could not do it.
However, she tried.
However she tried. [??]

In most instances, you can avoid the danger of forgetting the comma and spoiling the sense by substituting *but* for your initial *however's*. Put your *however's* (as conjunctive adverbs) within the sentence between commas: "She tried, however, a little longer."

With afterthoughts, the rule still holds—ordinarily you should set them off with a comma. But close sequences of cause and effect (even in openers) often make the comma optional with *for, because,* and *if,* and occasionally with others.

They stayed home for several reasons.
For several reasons they stayed home.
Everything was snug inside.
They wear few clothes because it never gets cold.
Punctuate accurately if you can.

It is a question of emphasis. A comma would have damaged none of them (when in doubt, follow the rule); it would merely have changed their rhetoric.

R U L E   I V .   *Enclose parenthetical insertions with a pair of commas.*

You are cutting the sentence in two, and inserting something necessary: if you do not tie off both ends, your thought will die on the table:

When he packs his bag, however he goes.
The car, an ancient Packard is still running.
April 10, 1980 is fine.

That handsome man in the ascot tie, is the groom.

John Jones, Jr. is wrong.

You do not mean that 1980 is fine, nor that Junior is wrong: all parenthetical insertions need a *pair* of commas:

The case, *nevertheless*, was closed.

She will see, *if she has any sense at all*, that he is right.

The same rule applies, of course, to *nonrestrictive* remarks, phrases, and clauses—all elements that are simply additive and hence parenthetical:

John, *my friend*, will do what he can.

The taxes, *which are reasonable*, will be paid.

New York, *where the buildings are tall*, is short of space.

That man, *who knows*, is not talking.

But restrictive phrases and clauses, which define and identify their antecedents and are thus integral extensions of them, should have no pair-of-commas (use *which* for nonrestrictive, *that* for restrictive; see p. 76):

The taxes that are reasonable will be paid.

The man who knows is not talking.

Again the linguists can help us. When we mean *the man who knows*, we say it all as a unit, all on the same level, with no change in stress and no "double-barred" pauses. When we mean *who knows* parenthetically, we add some stresses and put in the pauses:

/   /   /

The man, who knows, is not talking.

When *too* is in formal apposition, our stresses and pauses also mark it for commas:

Albert, too, likes to dance.

But *too* is often an integral extension of the word it modifies, and as such takes no commas:

He too can dance.

Commas are often optional. The difference between taking a phrase restrictively or nonrestrictively may be very slight, but use *pairs* of commas or none at all. Your meaning will dictate your choice.

Never separate subject and verb, or verb and object, with just one comma.

Some finer points. One comma of a pair enclosing an inserted remark may coincide with, and, in a sense, overlay, a comma "already there":

> In each box, a bottle was broken.
> In each box, however, a bottle was broken.

> The team lost, and the school was sick.
> The team lost, in spite of all, and the school was sick.

> The program will work, but the cost is high.
> The program will work, of course, but the cost is high.

Between the coordinate clauses, however, a semicolon would be clearer:

> The team lost, in spite of all; and the school was sick.

Beware: *however,* between commas, cannot substitute for *but.* You will be using a comma where a full stop (period or semicolon) should be.

Wrong:
> He wore a hat, however, it looked terrible.

Right (notice the two meanings):
> He wore a hat; however, it looked terrible.
> He wore a hat, however; it looked terrible.

Another point. *But* may absorb the first comma of a pair enclosing an introductory remark (although it need not do so):

> At any rate, he went.
> But, at any rate, he went.
> But at any rate, he went.
> But [,] if we want another party, we had better clean up.
> The party was a success, but [,] if we want another one, we had better clean up.

One final point, about typography. Put the comma *inside* all quotation marks:

> "He is a nut," she said.
> She called him a "nut," and walked away.

THE SEMICOLON

Use the semicolon where you could also use a period. Confusion comes from the belief that the semicolon is either a weak colon or a strong comma. It is most effective as neither. It is best as a kind of light period, a separator of contrasts. *Never* use it as a colon: its effect is exactly opposite. A colon, as in the preceding sentence, is a green light; a semicolon, as in this sentence, is a stop sign.

Of course, you may occasionally need to unscramble a long line of phrases and clauses:

> You should see that the thought is full, the words well cleaned, the points adjusted; and then your sentence will be ready to go. (*Note that the period rule would still guide you here:* ". . . adjusted. And then . . . .")

> Composition is hard because we often must discover our ideas by writing them out, clarifying them on paper; because we must find the right words to convey our ideas, and what we feel about them; and because we must find a clear and reasonable order for ideas that the mind presents simultaneously.

But the semicolon is better when it pulls related sentences together:

> She liked him; he was good to her; he had money in the bank.

And better still when it pivots a contrast:

> Work when you work; play when you play.
> A semicolon is a stop sign; a colon, a green light.

PARENTHESIS AND DASH

The dash says aloud what the parenthesis whispers. Both enclose interruptions too long for a pair of commas to hold. The dash is the more useful—since whispering tends to annoy—and will remain useful only if not overused. Overdone, it can be a sign of ignorance, or of laziness. But a well-cultivated dash will give you the ultimate means of control and urbanity. It can serve as a conversational colon. It can set off a concluding phrase—for emphasis. It can bring long introductory matters to focus, as in Freud's sentence on page 41. It can insert a full sentence—a clause is really an incorporated sentence—directly next to a key word. It allows a structural complexity with all the tone and alacrity of talk. When one of a pair of dashes falls where a comma would be, it absorbs the comma:

> **If one wanted to go, he certainly could.**
> **If one wanted to go—whether he was invited or not—he certainly could.**

Not so with the semicolon:

> **He wanted to go—whether he was invited or not; she had more sense.**

To indicate the dash, type two hyphens- -flush against the words they separate- -not one hyphen between two spaces, nor a hyphen looking exactly like a hyphen.

Put commas and periods *outside* a parenthetical group of words (like this one). (But if you make an entire sentence parenthetical, put the period inside.)

BRACKETS

Brackets indicate your own words inserted or substituted within a quotation from someone else: "Byron had already suggested that [they] had killed John Keats." You have substituted "they" for "the gentleman of *The Quarterly Review*" to suit your own context; you do the same when you interpolate a word of explanation. *Do not use parentheses:* they mark the enclosed words as part of the original quotation. Don't claim innocence because your typewriter lacks brackets. Just leave spaces and draw them in later, or type slant lines and tip them with pencil or with the underliner on your "6" key:

$$ \mathcal{L} \cdot \cdot \mathcal{J} $$

QUOTATION MARKS

Put quotation marks around quotations that "run directly into your text" (like this), but *not* around quotations set off from the text and indented. Periods and commas go *inside* quotation marks; semicolons and colons go *outside*.

This was another "thorn in the side."

He thought that "seeing is believing," until today.

In Greece it was "know thyself"; in America it is "know thy neighbor."

He left after the "Hughes Affair": he could do nothing more.

Although logic seems to demand the period or comma outside the quotation marks, convention has put them inside for the sake of appearance, even when the sentence ends in a single quoted word or letter:

Clara Bow was said to have "It."

Mark it with "T."

If you have seen the periods and commas outside, you were reading a British book or a freshman paper.

If a phrase to be quoted already contains quotation marks, reduce the original double marks (") to single ones ('):

Original	Your quotation
The word "cue" is interesting.	He writes that the "word 'cue' is interesting."

Notice what happens when the quotation within your quotation falls at the end:

Original	Your quotation
The Japanese call albatross "aho dori."	Jones reports that the "Japanese call albatross 'aho dori'."

ELLIPSIS

(1) Use three spaced periods . . . (the ellipsis mark) when omitting something from a quotation. Do *not* use them in your own text in place of a dash, or in mere insouciance. (2) If you omit the end of a sentence, add the period . . . ✓ (3) If your omission falls after a completed sentence, add the ellipsis mark to the period already there✓. . . . I have put a check over the periods. Notice the difference in spacing. (4) If you omit something from the beginning of a sentence within a quotation, begin your ellipsis mark two spaces after the period just ahead, like this✓ . . . It is not so difficult. But note that each placement of the ellipsis mark means something different.

Here is an uncut passage, followed by a shortened version showing in succession the four kinds of ellipsis:

> To learn a language, learn as thoroughly as possible a few everyday sentences. This will educate your ear for all future pronunciations. It will give you a fundamental grasp of structure. Some of the details of grammar will begin to appear. It will give you confidence. If you go abroad, you can buy a newspaper and find your way back to the hotel.

To learn a language, learn $^{(1)}$ . . . a few everyday sentences. This will educate your ear $^{(2)}$ . . . . It will give you a fundamental grasp of structure. $^{(3)}$ . . . It will give you confidence. $^{(4)}$ . . . you can buy a newspaper and find your way back to the hotel.

APOSTROPHE

Add 's to form the singular possessive (*dog's life, Yeats's poems, Marx's ideas*), except for ancient classical names (*Mars' armor*). A few plurals also form the possessive by adding 's (*children's hour, men's room, women's pool, mice's holiday, sheep's bellwether*), but the common plural, ending in s, takes the apostrophe after the s (*ships' company, citizens' rights*).

Polysyllabic names ending in s usually follow the rule for plurals, which they resemble, and drop the possessive s (*Dickens' novels, Marivaux' plays, veterans' insurance*), but euphony and sense may still urge the final s: *Horace's satires, Catullus's villa, Adams's field*. The page may get too thick with double s's; on the other hand, you may prefer to distinguish Dickens from Dicken and Adams from Adam.

Possessive pronouns have no apostrophe: *hers, its, theirs, yours, whose, oneself*. Note that *it's* means *it is*, and that *who's* means *who is*.

E X E R C I S E S

1. Write three groups of three or four sentences, each group containing a rhetorical fragment that cannot be mistaken for a mistake.

2. Write a dozen pairs of sentences, using the six conjunctions *and, but, for, or, yet, still,* on the pattern:

> **He hunted the hills and . . . .**
> **He hunted the hills, and . . . .**

3. Run off five or six sentences with concluding double appositives which might look like parts of a simple series but which are not: "He loved to camp, to hunt and to fish."

4. Write four or five asyndetic sentences (see page 52), each with three clauses.

5. Master *however* by writing five or six groups of three sentences on the following pattern:

> **However she tried, she could not do it.**
> **She tried, however, a very long time.**
> **She tried; however, she could not do it.**

6. Write five or six pairs of sentences to practice enclosing parenthetical insertions within a pair of commas:

> **April 10 is fine.**
> **April 10, 1990, is fine.**
> **The taxes will be paid.**
> **The taxes, which are reasonable, will be paid.**

7. Do the same with dashes and with parentheses.

8. Write six pairs of sentences showing the difference between nonrestrictive and restrictive clauses on the pattern:

> **The taxes, which are reasonable, will be paid.**
> **The taxes that are reasonable will be paid.**

9. Write six compound sentences, using a semicolon between two contrasting independent clauses.

6 / Words

HERE IS the word. Sesquipedalian or short, magniloquent or low, Latin or Anglo-Saxon, Celtic, Danish, French, Spanish, Indian, Hindustani, Dutch, Italian, Portuguese, Chinese, Hebrew, Turkish, Greek—a million words at our disposal, if we are disposed to use them. Although no language is richer than English, our average expository vocabularies are probably less than 8,000 words. We could all increase our active vocabularies; we all have a way to go to possess our inheritance.

VOCABULARY

If you can increase your hoard, you increase your chances of finding the right word, *le mot juste,* when you need it. Read as widely as you can, and look words up the second or third time you meet them. I once knew a man who swore he learned three new words a day from his reading by using each at least once in conversation. I didn't ask him about *polyphiloprogenitive* or *antidisestablishmentarianism.* It depends a little on the crowd. But the idea is sound. The bigger the vocabulary the more the ideas one can get across with it, the more the shades and intensities of meaning.

The big vocabulary also needs the little word. The vocabularian often strands himself on a Roman cloud and forgets the Anglo-Saxon ground—the common ground between him and his audience. So do not forget the little things, the *stuff, lint, get, twig, snap, go, mud, coax.* Hundreds of small words not in immediate vogue can refresh your vocabulary. There are the Norse and Anglo-Saxon adjectives in -y (*muggy, scrawny, drowsy*), for instance, which rarely appear in sober print. Conversely, the minute the beginner tries to sound dignified, in comes a misty layer of words a few feet off the ground and nowhere near heaven, the same two dozen or so, most of them verbs. One or two will do no harm, but any accumulation is fatal—words like *depart* instead of *go:*

accompany—go with	place—put
appeared—looked *or* seemed	possess—have
arrive—come	prepare—get ready
attempt—try	questioned—asked
become—get	receive—get
cause—make	relate—tell
cease—stop	remain—stay
complete—finish	remove—take off
continue—keep on	retire—go to bed
delve—dig	return—go back
discover—find	secure—get
locate—find	transform—turn

I add one treasured noun: *manner—way.* The question, as always, is one of meaning. *Manner* is something with a flourish; *way* is the usual way. But you will not find a normal *way* from one end of the university to the other. "She *placed* her cigarettes on the table" is usually not what the writer means. *Delve* is something that happens only when students begin to meditate. *Get* and *got* may be too colloquial for constant use in writing, but a discreet one or two can limber many a stiff sentence. Therefore, use the elegant Latin and the commonplace Anglo-Saxon, tastefully fitted; but shun the frayed gentility of *secure* and *place* and *remain.* You can find the shades of meaning in your dictionary.

Abraham Lincoln read the dictionary. You really can browse it with pleasure, looking at the pictures and finding out about aardvarks and axolotyles, jerboas and jerkins. You can amaze yourself at the number of things *set* can mean. Best of all, you can look at a word's derivation and get a quick sense of our linguistic history, of families of words and ideas, of how some meanings have changed and how some have persisted through centuries and across continents. *Mid,* for instance, is still what it has been for the last 5,000 years, persisting in most of the Indo-European languages all the way from Old Norse to Sanskrit and giving English a whole family of words from *middle* to *intermezzo.* Acquaintance with a family can make you feel at home. You can know and use a *ramp,* or a *rampage,* or a lion *rampant* familiarly, once you see the Old French for *climb* in all three. You can cut your meaning close to the old root, as in "He was *enduring* and *hard* as nails," where the Latin *durus* ("hard") has suggested its Anglo-Saxon synonym and given you a phrase your readers will like, though most of them won't know why.

Through the centuries, English has added Latin derivatives alongside the Anglo-Saxon words already there, keeping the old with the new: after the Anglo-Saxon *deor* (*deer*) came the *beast* and then the *brute,* from Latin through French, and the *animal* straight from Rome. Well over half our total vocabulary comes one way or another from Latin, although we use more Anglo-Saxon in assembling our sentences (*to, by, with, though, is*). The things of this world tend to be Anglo-Saxon (*man, house, stone, wind, rain*); the abstract qualities, Latin and French (*value, duty, contemplation*).

Our big words are Latin and Greek. Your reading will get you acquainted; your dictionary will show you their prefixes and roots. Learn the common ones (see Exercises, this section), and you can handle all kinds of foreigners at first encounter: *con-cession* (going along with), *ex-clude* (lock out), *pre-fer* (carry before), *sub-version* (turning under), *trans-late* (carry across), *claustro-phobia* (dread of being locked in), *hydro-phobia* (dread of water), *leuro-philia* (love of cats), *megalo-cephalic* (big-headed), *micro-meter* (little-measurer). You can even, for fun, coin a word to suit the occasion: *megalopede* (big-footed). You can remember that *intra-mural* means "within the (college) walls," and that "intermural sports," which is the frequent mispronunciation 'and misspelling, would mean something like "wall battling wall," a physical absurdity.

Besides the dictionary, you should own Roget's *Thesaurus,* the treasury of synonyms ("together-names"), in which you can find the word you couldn't think of, and all the shades of good and bad you want, from *pants* through *trousers* to *galligaskins.* Peter Roget's great work of 1852, compiled for fifty years and since augmented and refined, is indeed a treasury. Any one word will open the door. And once the writer sees all the resources, all the related words, "an instinctive tact," as Roget says, "will rarely fail to lead him to the proper choice." Checking for meaning in a dictionary will assure that your instincts are sound.

Learn to spell the words you use. The dictionary is your best friend, in the presence of your enemies, but three underlying principles and some tricks of the trade can help immeasurably:

PRINCIPLE 1. Letters represent sounds: proNUNciation can help you spell. No one proNOUNcing his words would make the familiar errors of "similiar" and "enviorment." You can even improve your social standing by learning to say *envIRONment* and *goverNment* and *FebRUary* and *intRAmural.* Simply sound out the letters. You can even say "convert*i*ble" and "indel*i*ble" and "plaus*i*ble" without sounding like a fool, and you can silently stress the *able* in words like "prob*able*" and "immov*able*" to remember the difficult distinction between words ending in *-ible,* and *-able.*

Consonants reliably represent their sounds. Remember that *c* and *g* go soft before *i* and *e.* Consequently you must add a *k* when extending words like *picnic* and *mimic—picnicKing, mimicKing* —to keep them from rhyming with *slicing* or *dicing.* Conversely, you just keep the *e* (where you would normally drop it) when making *peace* into *peacEable* and *change* into *changEable.*

Single *s* is pronounced *zh* in words like *vision, occasion, pleasure.* Knowing that *ss* hisses will keep you from errors like *occassion,* which would sound like *passion.*

Vowels sound short and light before single consonants: *hat, pet, mit, hop, mut.* When you add any vowel (including *y*) the first vowel will say its name: *hate, Pete, mite, hoping, mutable.* Notice how the *a* in *-able* keeps the main vowel saying its name in words like *unmistakable, likable,* and *notable.* Therefore, to keep a vowel short, protect it with a double consonant: *petting, hopping.* This explains the troublesome *rr* in *occuRRence:* a single *r* would make it say *cure* in the middle. *Putting* a golf ball and *putting* something on paper must both use *tt* to keep from being pronounced *pewting.* Compare *stony* with *sonny* and *bony* with *bonny.* The *y* is replacing the *e* in *stone* and *bone,* and the rule is working perfectly. It works in any accented syllable: compare *forgeTTable* with *mar-*

keTing, and *begiNNing* with *buttoNing,* and *compeLLing* with *traveLing.*

Likewise, when *full* combines and loses its stress, it also loses an *l.* Note the single and double *l* in *fulFILLment.* Similarly, *SOULful, GRATEful, AWful*—even *SPOONful.*

PRINCIPLE II. The two sounds for *c* account for the second principle, the old rule:

> *I* before *e*
> **Except after *c*,**
> **Or when sounded like *a***
> **As in *neighbor* and *weigh.***

It works like a charm (*achieve, believe; receive, conceive*). Remember that *leisure* was once pronounced "lay-sure," and *foreign,* "forayn." Memorize these important exceptions: *seize, weird, either, sheik, forfeit, counterfeit.* Note that all are pronounced "ee" (with a little crowding) and that the *e* comes first. Then note that another small group goes the opposite way, having a long *i* sound as in the German "Heil"; *height, sleight, seismograph, kaleidoscope. Financier,* another exception, follows its French origin and its original sound.

PRINCIPLE III. Most big words follow the Latin or French from which they came (and consequently spell their sounds letter for letter). Look up the derivations of the words you misspell (note that double *s,* and explain it). You will never again have trouble with *desperate* and *separate* once you discover that the first comes from *de-spero,* "without hope," and that se*PAR*ate divides equals, as PAR in golf. Nor with *definite* or *definitive* once you see the kinship of both with *finite* and *finish.* Derivations can also help you a little with the devilment of *-able* and *-ible,* since, except for a few ringers, the *i* remains from Latin, and the *-ables* are either French (*ami-able*) or Anglo-Saxon copies (*workable*). Knowing origins can help at crucial points: *resemblAnce* comes from Latin *simulAre,* "to copy"; *existEnce* comes from *Latin existEre,* "to stand forth."

The biggest help comes from learning the common Latin prefixes, which by a process of assimilation (*ad-similis,* "*like to like*") account for the double consonants at the first syLLabic joint of so many of our words:

AD- (toward, to): *abbreviate* (shorten down), *accept* (grasp to).

CON- (with): *collapse* (fall with), *commit* (send with).

DIS- (apart): *dissect* (cut apart), *dissolve* (loosen apart).

IN- (into): *illuminate* (shine into), *illusion* (playing into).

IN- (not): *illegal* (not lawful), *immature* (not ripe).

INTER- (between): *interrupt* (break between), *interrogate* (ask between).

OB- (towards, to): *occupy* (take in), *oppose* (put to), *offer* (carry to).

SUB- (under): *suffer* (bear under), *suppose* (put down).

SYN- ("together"—this one is Greek): *symmetry* (measuring together), *syllogism* (logic together).

Spelling takes a will, an eye, and an ear. And a dictionary. Keep a list of your favorite enemies. Memorize one or two a day. Write them in the air in longhand. Visualize them. Imagine a blinking neon sign, with the wicked letters red and tall—d e f i n I t e—d e f i n I t e. Then print them once, write them twice, and blink them a few times more as you go to sleep. But best of all, make up whatever devices you can—the crazier the better—to remember the tricky parts:

DANCE attenDANCE.

ExistENCE is TENSE.

There's IRON in this enviRONment.

The resisTANCE took its STANCE.

There's an ANT on the defendANT.

LOOSE as a goose.

LOSE loses an O.

ALLOT isn't A LOT.

Already isn't ALL RIGHT.

I for gaiety.

The LL in paraLLel gives me el.

PURr in PURsuit.

Here are some more of the perpetual headaches:

accept—except
accommodate
acknowledgment—judgment
advice—advise
affect—effect
allusion—illusion—disillusion
analysis—analyzing—annual

apologize
arrangement—argument
businessman
capital—capitol
careful—successful—fulfillment
challenge
cite—site—insight

committee
complement—compliment—
    supplement
curriculum—career—occurrence
decide—divide—devices
desert—dessert
despair—desperate—separate
detrimental—dealt
dilemma—condemn
disastrous
embarrassment
eminent—imminent—immanent
exaggerate
explanation

forward—foreword
genius—ingenious
height—eighth
hypocrisy—democracy
irritable
lonely—loneliness
Negroes—heroes—tomatoes
obstacle
operate (opus, opera)
possession
primitive
principal—principle
proceed—precede—procedure
until—till

Check your capitals. You know about sentences and names, certainly; but the following points are troublesome. Capitalize:

1. Names of races and languages—Negro, Indian, French, English.

2. North, south, east, and west ONLY WHEN THEY ARE REGIONS —the mysterious East, the new Southwest.

3. The COMPLETE names of churches, rivers, hotels, and the like—the First Baptist Church, the Mark Hopkins Hotel, the Suwannee River.

4. All words in titles, except prepositions, articles, and conjunctions. But capitalize even these if they come first or last, or if they are longer than five letters—"I'm Through with Love," *Gone with the Wind*, "I'll Stand By," *In Darkest Africa*. Capitalize nouns, adjectives, and prefixes in hyphenated compounds—*The Eighteenth-Century Background*, *The Anti-Idealist* (but *The Antislavery Movement*). With magazines and newspapers only, drop the *The* as part of the title (the *Saturday Evening Post*, the Kansas City *Star*—note that only *Star*, or *Tribune*, or *Times* is treated as the newspaper's proper title).

5. References to a specific section of a work—the Index, his Preface, Chapter 1, Act II, Scene iii, Volume IV.

6. Abstract nouns, when you want emphasis, serious or humorous—". . . the truths contradict, so what is Truth?"; Very Important Person; the Ideal.

DO NOT capitalize the seasons—spring, winter, midsummer.

DO NOT capitalize after a colon, unless what follows is a quotation beginning with a capital.

ABSTRACT AND CONCRETE

An understanding of the distinction between abstract and concrete words lies at the center of any style. Tangible, touchable things are "concrete"; their qualities, along with all our emotional, intellectual, and spiritual states, are "abstract." The rule for a good style is to be as concrete as you can, to illustrate tangibly your general propositions, to use *shoes* and *ships* and *sealing wax* instead of *commercial concomitants*. You risk being childish, but the risk is slight indeed: our minds so crave abstraction we can hardly pin them down to specifics.

Abstraction, a "drawing out from," is the very nature of thought. Thought moves from concrete to abstract. In fact, *all* words are abstractions. *Stick* is a generalization of all sticks, the crooked and the straight, the long and the short, the peeled and the shaggy. No word fits its object like a glove, because words are not things: words represent ideas of things. They are the means by which we class eggs and tents and trees, and hence can handle them as ideas —not as actual things but as *kinds* of things. A man could hold an egg in his hand, but he could not think about it, or talk about it, unless he had some larger idea with which his mind, too, could grasp it, some idea like *thing*, or *throwing thing*, or *egg*—which would class this one white spheroid with all the eggs he knew, from ostrich to hummingbird, with the *idea* of egg. One word per item would be useless, would be no idea at all.

So before we disparage abstraction, we should understand that it is an essential distillation, a primary and natural and continual mental process. We cannot do without it. We could not make four of two and two. So we make abstractions of abstractions to handle bigger and bigger groups of ideas. *Egg* becomes *food*, and *food* becomes *nourishment*. We also classify all the psychic and physical qualities we can recognize: *candor, truth, anger, beauty, negligence, temperament*. But because our thoughts drift upward, we need always to look for the word that will bring them nearer earth, that will make our abstractions seem visible and tangible, that will make them graspable. We have to put them in reach of our reader's own busily abstracting headpiece.

We must pin our abstractions down with constant comparisons with the concrete eggs from which they sprang. I might have written that sentence—as I found myself starting to do: "Abstractions should be actualized by a process of constant comparisons with the concrete objects which they represent." Note what I have done to pull this down within reach. First, I have used *we;* that is, you and me, real people. I have also cut the inhuman passive voice to put us in the act. Then I have changed *actualize* to *pin down,* a visible act that, being commonplace and proverbial, makes us feel at home among the abstractions. I have replaced the abstract *by a process of* with its simpler abstract equivalent *with.* More important, I have made *eggs* stand for all objects—and note how easily our abstracters take this in. Furthermore, I have punned on *concrete,* making it, for a fleeting instant, into cement. How? By choosing *egg,* something that could really be made out of concrete, instead of *stick* (which I had first put there): a concrete stick is not much as a physical possibility. Finally, I have gone on to use *egg* also as a real egg by having the abstract ideas spring from it. Later, I almost changed *sprang* to *hatched,* but decided that this was too vivid. It would make the concrete egg too nearly real, and the picture of broken cement with fluffy abstractions peeping forth would have gotten in the way of the idea—that is, the disembodied abstract concept—I was trying to convey.

Metaphor

In fact, I have been using metaphors. There is no more useful way of making our abstractions concrete. The word is Greek for "transfer" (*meta* equals *trans* equals *across; phor* equals *fer* equals *ferry*). The idea is that of representing something as if it were something else, objects as if all of them were eggs, abstractions as if they were chickens that are also vaguely like flowers springing, thought as if it were rising steam. Metaphors illustrate, in a word, our general ideas. I might have written at length about how an idea is like an egg. I did, in fact, follow each declaration with an example, and I illustrated the point with a man holding an egg. But the metaphor makes the comparison at a stroke. I used our common word *grasp* for "understanding," comparing the mind to something with hands, *transferring* the physical picture of the clutching hand to the invisible mental act.

Almost all our words are metaphors, usually with the physical picture faded. *Transfer* itself pictures a physical portage. When the company *transfers* its men it is sending them about the country as if by piggyback, or raft, or whatever. But mercifully the physical facts have faded, and we can use the word in comfortable abstraction. Now, precisely because we are constantly abstracting, constantly letting the picture fade, you can use metaphor to great advantage—or disastrously, if your eyes aren't sharp. With metaphors you avoid the unpictorial quality of most of our writing; you make your writing both vivid and unique. As Aristotle said, the metaphor is clear, agreeable, and strange; like a solved riddle, it is the most delightful of teachers.

It seems to me that there are four levels of metaphor, each with a different clarity and force (and, as you will see, we must here distinguish between the general idea of "metaphor" as the whole process of transfer, and that specific thing called "a metaphor"):

> *Simile:* She was *like* a horse.
> She stopped *as* a horse stops.
> She stopped *as if* she were a horse.
> *Metaphor:* She was a horse.
> *Implied metaphor:* She snorted and tossed her mane.
> *Dead metaphor:* She bridled.

The simile is the most obvious of the forms the metaphor can take, and hence would seem elementary. But it has powers of its own, particularly in its *as if* variation, where the writer seems to be trying urgently to express the inexpressible, comparing his subject to several different possibilities, no one wholly adequate. The simile has a high poetic energy. D. H. Lawrence uses it frequently, as in the following paragraph from *The Plumed Serpent* (my italics):

> The lake was quite black, *like a great pit.* The wind suddenly blew with violence, with a strange ripping sound in the mango trees, *as if some membrane in the air were being ripped.* The white-flowered oleanders in the garden below leaned over quite flat, their white flowers ghostly, going right down to the earth,

in the pale beam of the lamp—*like a street lamp*—that shone on
the wall at the front entrance.

The plain metaphor makes the comparison in one imaginative
leap. It is shorthand for "as if she were a horse"; it pretends, by
exaggeration (*hyperbole*), that she is, in fact, a horse. The effect
is sometimes humorous or bitter, but can be simply and aptly visual:
"The road was a ribbon of silver."

The implied metaphor is the most widely useful. It operates
most frequently among the verbs, as in *snorted* and *tossed*, the
horsy verbs suggesting "horse." Most ideas can suggest analogues
of physical processes or natural history. Give your television system *tentacles*, and you have compared TV to an octopus, with all
its lethal and wiry suggestions. You can have your school spirit
fall below zero. You can even pun on the physical Latin com-
ponents in our abstract words, turning them back into their original
suggestions of physical acts, as in "The *enterprise* grabbed everything" (some beast or army is rushing in), for *enterprise* means in
Latin something like "to rush in and grab." Too subtle? No, the
contrast between *enterprise* and *grabbed* will please anyone, and
the few who see it all will be delighted.

Enterprise is really a dead metaphor, and the art of resuscita-
tion is the metaphorist's finest skill. It comes from liking words,
and paying attention to what they say. The punster makes the
writer, if he can restrain himself. Simply add onto the dead metaphor enough implied metaphors to get the circulation going again:
She bridled, snorting and tossing her mane. *She bridled* means, by
itself, as we have abstracted it, nothing more than "reacted
disdainfully." By bringing the metaphor back to life, we keep the
general meaning but also restore the physical picture of a horse
lifting its head and arching its neck against the bridle. It is ex-
hilarating. We recognize *bridle* concretely and truly for the first
time. We know the word, and we know the woman. We have an
image of her, a posture vaguely suggestive of a horse.

Perhaps the best dead metaphors to revive are those in proverbial clichés. See what Thoreau does (in his journal) with *spur
of the moment:*

**I feel the spur of the moment thrust deep into my side. The
present is an inexorable rider.**

Or again, when in *Walden* he speaks of wanting "to improve the nick of time, and notch it on my stick too," and of not being *thrown off the track* "by every nutshell and mosquito's wing that falls on the rails." In each case he takes the proverbial phrase literally and physically, adding an attribute or two to bring the old metaphor back alive.

You can go too far, of course. The metaphors can be too thick and vivid, and the obvious pun brings a howl of protest. Jane Austen disliked metaphors, as Mary Laselles notes (*Jane Austen and Her Art,* pp. 111–12), and reserved them for her hollow characters. I myself have advised scholars not to use them because they are so often overworked and so often tangled in physical impossibilities. "The violent population explosion has paved the way for new intellectual growth" looks pretty good—until you realize that explosions do not pave, and that new vegetation does not grow up through pavement. The metaphor, then, is your most potent device. It makes your thoughts concrete, and your writing vivid. It tells in an instant how your subject looks to you. But it is dangerous. It should be quiet, almost unnoticed, with all details agreeing and all absolutely consistent with the natural universe.

ALLUSION

Allusions also illustrate your general idea by referring it to something else, making it take your reader as Grant took Richmond, making you the Mickey Mantle of the essay, or the Mickey Mouse. Of Albert Camus, the Nobel Prize-winning French author, William Bittner writes (*Atlantic Monthly,* February, 1961): "he looked . . . like a Japanese Humphrey Bogart." Allusions depend on common knowledge. Like the metaphor they make a sudden familiar illustration of the remote. Perhaps the most effective ones depend on a knowledge of literature. When Thoreau writes that "the winter of man's discontent was thawing as well as the earth," we get a secret pleasure from recognizing this as an allusive borrowing from the opening lines of Shakespeare's *Richard III:* "Now is the winter of our discontent/Made glorious summer by this sun of York." Thoreau flatters us by assuming that we are as well read as he. We do not need to catch the allusion to enjoy his point, but if we get it, we do feel a sudden fellowship of knowledge with him. We now see the full metaphorical force, in Thoreau as in

Shakespeare; and it is pointed by our remembrance of the whole of Richard Crookback's twisted discontent, an allusive illustration of all our pitiful resentments now thawing with the spring.

DICTION

"What we need is a mixed diction," said Aristotle, and his point remains true twenty-three centuries and several languages later. The aim of style, he says, is to be clear but distinguished. For clarity we need common, current words; but used alone, these are commonplace, and as ephemeral as everyday talk. For distinction we need unusual words, those not heard every minute, strange words, foreign words, metaphors; but used alone, these become gibberish. What we need is a diction that marries the popular with the dignified, the clear current with the sedgy margins of language and thought.

Not too low, not too high; not too simple, not too hard—an easy breadth of idea and vocabulary. English is peculiarly well endowed for this Aristotelian mixture. The long abstract Latin words and the short concrete Anglo-Saxon ones give you all the range you need. For most of your ideas you can find Latin and Anglo-Saxon partners. In fact, for many ideas you can find a whole spectrum of synonyms from Latin through French to Anglo-Saxon, from general to specific: *intrepidity, fortitude, valor, courage, bravery, pluck, guts.* You can choose the high word for high effect, or you can get tough with Anglo-Saxon specifics. But you do not want all Anglo-Saxon, and you must especially guard against sobriety's luring you into all Latin. Tune your diction agreeably between the two extremes.

The mixing of Latin and Anglo-Saxon, as John Crowe Ransom has noted, is what gives Shakespeare much of his power:

> **This my hand will rather**
> **The multitudinous seas incarnadine,**
> **Making the green one red.**

The short Anglo-Saxon *seas* works sharply between the two magnificent Latin words, as do the three short Anglo-Saxons that bring the big passage to rest, contrasting the Anglo-Saxon *red* with its big Latin synonym, *incarnadine.* William Faulkner, who has soaked himself in Shakespeare, gets much the same power from the same mixture. He is describing a very old Negro woman in *The Sound and the Fury* (the title itself comes from Shakespeare's *Macbeth*, the source of the *multitudinous seas* passage). She has been fat, but now she is wrinkled and completely shrunken except for her stomach:

> . . . a paunch almost dropsical, as though muscle and tissue had been courage or fortitude which the days or the years had consumed until only the indomitable skeleton was left rising like a ruin or a landmark above the somnolent and impervious guts . . . .

The impact of that short, ugly Anglo-Saxon word, with its slang metaphorical pun, is almost unbearably moving. And the impact would be nothing, the effect slurring, without the grand Latin preparation. "What we need is a mixed diction."

Beware of wordiness. Verbosity is a disease. Symptoms—severe inflation of the language, difficulty in following the point, extreme drowsiness. Cause—too much Latin and the passive voice (see pp. 27–29). Cure—making words count, and administering moderate doses of Anglo-Saxon. In speaking of sentences earlier, I commended elaboration. Now I shall recommend deletion. A fully worded sentence, each word in place and pulling its weight, is a joy to see. But a sentence full of words is not. Words should count. And the best way to make them count is to count the words in each suspicious case. Any shorter version will be clearer. I once counted the words, sentence by sentence, in a thirty-page manuscript rejected as "too loose." In some sentences I cut no more than one or two words. I rephrased many, but I think I cut no entire sentence. In fact, I added a considerable paragraph; and I still had five pages fewer, and a better essay.

Sentences can be too short and dense, of course. Many thoughts need explanation and an example or two. Many need the airing of *and*'s and *of*'s. Many simply need some loosening of phrase. In fact, colloquial phrasing, which is as clear and unnoticed as a clean window, is usually longer than its formal equivalent: *something to eat* as compared to *dinner*. By all counts, *dinner* should be better. It is shorter. It is more precise. Yet *something to eat* has social delicacy (at least as I am imagining the party). "Shall we have something to eat?" is more polite than the more economical

"Shall we have dinner?" We don't want to push our friends around with precise and economic suggestions. We want them at their ease, with the choices slightly vague. Consequently, when we write *what we are after* for *object* and *how it is done* for *method,* we give our all-too-chilly prose some social warmth. These colloquial phrases use more words, but they are not wordy if they pull with the rest of the sentence.

Beware the of-and-which disease. Overusing *of's* and *which's* is another common verbal malady. Diagnosis: a frequent result of formality and the passive voice, though often present in the most active sentences. Something like sleeping sickness. *With's, in's, to's,* and *by's* also inflamed. Surgery imperative. Here is a typical, and actual, case:

> Many biological journals, especially those *which* regularly publish new scientific names, now state *in* each issue the exact date *of* publication *of* the preceding issue. *In* dealing *with* journals *which* do not follow this practice, or *with* volumes *which* are issued individually, the biologist often needs *to* resort *to* indexes . . . *in order to* determine the actual date *of* publication *of* a particular name.

Note *of publication of* twice over, and the three *which's.* The passage is a sleeping beauty. The longer you look at it the more useless little attendants you see. Note the inevitable passive voice (*which are issued*) in spite of the author's active efforts. The *of's* accompany extra nouns, *publication* repeating *publish,* for instance. Remedy: (1) eliminate *of's* and their nouns, (2) change *which-*clauses into participles, (3) change nouns into verbs. You can cut more than a third of this passage without touching the sense (using 39 words instead of 63):

> Many biological journals, especially those regularly *publishing* new scientific names, now give the date of each preceding issue. With journals not *following* this practice, and with some books, the biologist must turn to indexes . . . *to date* a particular name.

You can cut most *which's,* one way or another, with no loss of blood. Participles can modify their antecedents directly, since they are verbal adjectives, without an intervening *which:* "a car *which was* going south" is "a car going south." Similarly with the adjective itself: "a song *which was* popular last year" is "a song popular last year." Beware of this whole crowd: *who are, that was, which are.*

If you need a relative clause, remember *that. Which* has almost completely displaced it in labored writing. *That* is still best for restrictive clauses, those necessary to definition: "A house that faces north is cool" (a participle would save a word: "A house facing north is cool"). *That* is tolerable; *which* is downright oppressive. *Which* should signal the nonrestrictive clause (the afterthought): "The house, which faces north, is a good buy." Here you need *which.* Even restrictive clauses must turn to *which* when complicated parallels arise. "He preaches the brotherhood of man *that* everyone affirms" elaborates like this: "He preaches the brotherhood of man *which* everyone affirms, *which* all the great philosophies support, but *for which* few can make any immediate concession." Nevertheless, if you need relatives, a *that* will often ease your sentences and save you from the *which*'s.

Verbs and their derivatives, especially present participles and gerunds, can also help to cure a string of *of*'s. Alfred North Whitehead, usually of clear mind, once produced this linked sausage: "Education is the acquisition *of* the art *of* the utilization *of* knowledge." Anything to get around the three *of*'s and the three heavy nouns would have been better: "Education is the art of learning to use knowledge." I have replaced *the acquisition of* with *learning,* and *the utilization of* with *to use.* Shun the *-tion*'s! Simply change your surplus *-tion*'s and *of*'s—along with your *which*-phrases —into verbs (*to use*) or verbals (*learning*). You will save words, and activate your sentences.

Break the noun habit.   English has always used nouns as adjectives, as in "*rail*road," "*railroad* station," "*court* house," and "*noun* habit." But modern prose has aggravated the tendency beyond belief; and we get such monstrosities as *child sex education course,* whole strings of nothing but nouns. Professors of education, sociology, and psychology are the worst noun stringers, the hardest for you not to copy if you take their courses. But we have all caught the habit. The nouns *level* and *quality* have produced a rash of redundancies. A meeting of "high officials" has now unfortunately become a meeting of "high-*level* officials." The "finest cloth" these days is always "finest *quality* cloth." Drop those two redundant clichés, and you will make a good start, and will sound surprisingly original. You can drop many an excess noun:

Wrong	*Right*
advance notice	notice
long in size	long
puzzling in nature	puzzling
of an indefinite nature	indefinite
of a peculiar kind	peculiar
in order to	to
by means of	by
in relation to	with
in connection with	with
1962-model car	1962 car

Wherever possible find the equivalent adjective:

of great importance	important
highest significance level	highest significant level
government spending	governmental spending
reaction fixation	reactional fixation
sex education	sexual education
teaching excellence	excellent teaching
encourage teaching quality	encourage good teaching

Or change the noun to its related participle:

advance placement	advanced placement
color film	colored film
uniform police	uniformed police
poison arrow	poisoned arrow

Or make the noun possessive:

reader interest	reader's interest
factory worker wage	factory worker's wage
veterans insurance	veterans' insurance

Or use a cautious *of:*

Wrong	*Right*
color lipstick	color of lipstick
teaching science	science of pedagogy
production quality	quality of production
high quality program	program of high quality
significance level	level of significance
a Marxist-type program	a Marxist program *or*
	a Marxist type of program

Of all our misused nouns, *type* has become peculiarly pestilential and trite. Advertisers talk of *detergent-type cleansers* instead of *detergents;* educators, of *apprentice-type situations* instead of *apprenticeships;* newspapermen, of *fascist-type organizations* instead of *fascistic organizations.* Don't copy your seniors; write boldly. We have become a nation of hairsplitters, afraid of saying *Czechoslovakia's Russian tanks* for fear that the reader will think they really belong to Russia. So the reporter writes *Russian-type tanks,* making an unnecessary distinction, and cluttering the page with one more *type-type* expression. We have forgotten that making the individual stand for the type is the simplest and oldest of metaphors: "Give us this day our daily bread." A twentieth-century writer might have thought it necessary to say "bread-type food."

It all comes down to redundancy, the clutter of useless words and tangential ideas—"the accumulation of words that add nothing to the sense and cloud up what clarity there is," as Aristotle says. What we write should be easy to read. Too many distinctions, too many nouns, and too much Latin can be pea soup:

> **Reading is a processing skill of symbolic reasoning sustained by the interfacilitation of an intricate hierarchy of substrata factors that have been mobilized as a psychological working system and pressed into service in accordance with the purpose of the reader.**

This comes from an educator, with the wrong kind of education. He is saying:

> **Reading is a process of symbolic reasoning aided by an intricate network of ideas and motives.**

Try *not* to define your terms. If you do, you are probably either evading the toil of finding the right word, or defining the obvious:

> **Let us agree to use the word signal as an abbreviation for the phrase "the simplest kind of sign." (This agrees fairly well with the customary meaning of the word "signal.")**

Now, really! That came from a renowned semanticist, a student of the meanings of words. The customary meaning of a word *is* its meaning, and uncustomary meanings come only from careful punning. Don't underestimate your readers, as this semanticist did.

The definer of words is usually a bad writer. Our semanticist continues, trying to get his signals straight and grinding out about three parts sawdust to every one of meat. In the following excerpt, the italics are his; the brackets, mine. Read the sentence first as it was written; then read it again, omitting the bracketed words:

> **The moral of such examples is that *all intelligent criticism* [*of any instance*] *of language* [*in use*] *must begin with understanding* [*of*] *the motives* [*and purposes*] *of the speaker* [*in that situation*].**

Here, each of the bracketed phrases is already implied in the others. Attempting to be precise, the writer has beclouded himself. Naturally the speaker would be "in that situation"; naturally a sampling of language would be "an instance" of language "in use." *Motives* may not be *purposes,* but the difference here is insignificant. Our semanticist's next sentence deserves some kind of immortality. He means "Muddy language causes trouble":

> **Unfortunately, the type of case that causes trouble in practice is that in which the kind of use made of language is not transparently clear . . . .**

Clearly, it is hard to be transparent. Writing is hard. It requires constant attention to meanings, and constant pruning. It requires a diction a cut above the commonplace, a cut above the inaccuracies and circumlocutions of speech, yet within easy reach. Clarity is the first aim; economy, the second; grace, the third; dignity, the fourth. Our writing should be a little strange, a little out of the ordinary, a little beautiful, with words and phrases not met everyday but seeming as right and natural as grass. A good diction takes care and cultivation.

It can be overcultivated. It may seem to call attention to itself rather than to its subject. Suddenly we are aware of the writer at work. In the following passage I have italicized elements that individually may have a certain effectiveness, but that cumulatively become mannerism. Some are rudundant; some are trite. All is somehow cozy and grandiose, and a little too nautical. Note the final, glorious fragment.

There's little excitement *ashore* when merchant ships from *faraway* India, Nationalist China, or Egypt *knife through* the *gentle swells* of Virginia's Hampton Roads. This *unconcern* may simply reflect the *nonchalance* of people who live by *one of the world's great seaports.* Or perhaps *it's just* that *folk* who *dwell* in the *home towns* of atomic submarines and Mercury astronauts are not likely to be impressed by a visiting freighter, *from however distant a realm.* An apprentice seaman aboard one of these *vessels soon* learns that he is entering *no sleepy southern harbor.* Around him in *the Roads* itself *ride* naval vessels of many nations, *perhaps including his own.* The big gray warships *dwarf* the *tiny* sailing craft and motor boats that *dart* around the water *on a good day. Off to port lies* Norfolk, *home* of the largest naval operating base *on this globe*, NATO's North Atlantic headquarters. *Upstream a bit* and also *to port*, the mouth of the Elizabeth River leads to Portsmouth and a major naval shipyard. *To starboard lies* Hampton, where at Langley Air Force Base the National Aeronautics and Space Administration prepares to send a man *into the heavens.* Just beyond Hampton *looms* the *huge* steel framework of the Newport News Shipbuilding and Dry Dock Company, *from whose ways slide* the atom-powered surface and underseas warships *of tomorrow. All this and more* form today's *metropolitan complex* surrounding Hampton Roads—four large, booming cities *peopled* by more than a million *souls. It's a huge, sprawling* urban area, *engaged* more than ever in world commerce and *deeply involved* in the nation's defense. *Here is the resurgent south, making instead of awaiting its destiny,* a hundred years and *a world away* from the *day* when the Monitor and the Merrimac *battled clumsily* in Hampton Roads. And still further away in time, *if not entirely in temper,* from the *geographically nearby restored* Colonial Capital at Williamsburg, from Captain John Smith's Jamestown Island, from the Yorktown battlefield on which George Washington *accepted the sword of surrender* from Cornwallis.*

* Robert Damron, "Hampton Roads," *Voyager*, July–August, 1960, p. 124.

EXERCISES

1. Browse your dictionary and find half a dozen families of words, like *ramp-rampage-rampant*. Give the root-idea of each family, and a word or two in definition of each word.

2. Make a permanent reference list by looking up in your dictionary each of the Latin and Greek prefixes and constituents listed below. Illustrate each with several English derivatives closely translated, as in these two examples: *con-* (*with*)—convince (conquer with), conclude (shut with), concur (run with); *gyno-* (*woman*)—gynephobia (fear of women), gynecocracy (government by women).

LATIN: *a-* (*ab-*), *ad-*, *ante-*, *bene-*, *bi-*, *circum-*, *con-*, *contra-*, *di-* (*dis-*), *e-* (*ex-*), *in-* (two meanings), *inter-*, *intra-*, *mal-*, *multi-*, *ob-*, *per-*, *post-*, *pre-*, *pro-*, *retro-*, *semi-*, *sub-* (*sur-*), *super-*, *trans-*, *ultra-*.

GREEK: *a-* (*an-*), *-agogue*, *allo-*, *anthropo-*, *anti-*, *apo-*, *arch-*, *auto-*, *batho-*, *bio-*, *cata-*, *cephalo-*, *chron-*, *-cracy*, *demo-*, *dia-*, *dyna-*, *dys-*, *ecto-*, *epi-*, *eu-*, *-gen*, *geo-*, *-gon*, *-gony*, *graph-*, *gyn-*, *hemi-*, *hepta-*, *hetero-*, *hexa-*, *homo-*, *hydr-*, *hyper-*, *hypo-*, *log-*, *mega-*, *meter-*, *micro-*, *mono-*, *morph-*, *-nomy*, *-nym-*, *-pathy*, *penta-*, *-phag*, *phil-*, *-phobe*(*ia*), *-phone*, *poly-*, *pseudo-*, *psyche-*, *-scope*, *soph-*, *stero-*, *sym*(*n*)*-*, *tele-*, *tetera-*, *theo-*, *thermo-*, *tri-*, *zoo-*.

3. Think up and look up eight or nine words built on each of the following Latin verbs and their past participles:

agere, actus (do)—agent, act

audire, auditus (hear)—audit

caedere, cisus (cut, cut down)—precise

capere, captus (seize)—capable

cedere, cessus (go)—concede

claudere, clausus (shut)—close, include

currere, cursus (run)—recur, course

dicere, dictus (say)—dictate

ducere, ductus (lead)—produce

facere, factus (make)—infect

ferre, latus (carry)—infer, relate

fidere, fisus (trust)—confide, Fido

fundere, fusus (pour)—refuse, refund

gerere, gestus (bear, act)—belligerent, gesture

gradi, gressus (step)—grade, digressions

ire, itus (go)—exit, tradition
jacere, jactus (throw)—reject
legere, lectus (choose, read) —legible, elect
loqui, locutus (speak)—circumlocution
mittere, missus (send)—permit, mission
pellere, pulsus (drive)—impel, repulse
pendere, pensus (hang)—depend, pension
plicare, plicatus (fold)—implication, complex
ponere, positus (put)—response, position
portare, portatus (carry)— import
rumpere, ruptus (break)— rumpus, erupt

scribere, scriptus (write)— scribble, script
sedere, sessus (sit)—sedentary, assess
sentire, sensus (feel)—sense
specere, spectus (look)— speculate
tendere, tensus (stretch)— tend, tense
tenere, tentus (hold)—content
trahere, tractus (drag)— tractor
venire, ventus (come)—convene, invent
vertere, versus (turn)—diverting, verse
videre, visus (see)—divide, visible
vocare, vocatus (call)—vocation

4. Capitalize the following, and italicize where necessary:

go west, young man.
the east side of town
east side, west side
the methodist episcopal church
the missouri river
the new york public library
the tall negro spoke french.

she loved the spring.
health within seconds (book)
the logical-positive approach (book)
the country gentleman (magazine)
the saint louis post-dispatch (newspaper)

5. Make five series of words running from particular to general, as in *ripe peach, peach, drupaceous fruit, fruit, dessert, food, nourishment.*
6. Make five series of words running from low connotations to high (see pp. 73–74), drawing a line (when possible) where the Anglo-Saxon gives way to French or Latin. Start with *swine* and *stuck up* (meaning *conceited*). The abstract ideas will work best, and Roget's *Thesaurus* can be most helpful.
7. Write five sentences in which you use a concrete object to represent an entire abstract class, each sentence paired with its abstracted translation:

A *good steak* might have saved John Keats.
A *proper protein diet* might have saved John Keats.

8. Write five sentences in which you extend the metaphorical picture in common phrases such as *pin down, stick to, outline, count your chickens* ("She pinned him down methodically, each question sticking in a different place, until he couldn't wiggle out of it").

9. In your next essay, use a tactful *sweet as a nut, sharp as a tack*, and so forth, once on every page (see "Clichés," pp. 88–89).

10. Write five sets of sentences illustrating the four levels of metaphor (see p. 70).

11. Write five sentences in which you revive a dead metaphor.

12. Write five sentences in which you pun metaphorically on a Latin word: "The *enterprise grabbed* everything."

13. Write five sentences in which you couple a Latin adjective and an Anglo-Saxon noun, as in the phrase *inconsequential snip*.

14. Find in your textbooks two or three passages suffering from the *of*-and-*which* disease and the noun habit ("which shows the effect of age and intelligence level upon the emergence of child behavior difficulties") and rewrite them in clear English.

7 / Usage

USAGE IS "the way they say it." Usage provides the current, it keeps us afloat, it keeps us fresh—as it sweeps us along. But to distinguish himself the writer must always battle it, must always swim upstream. He may say, "Hooja-eatwith?"; but he will write: "With whom did they compare themselves? With the best, with whoever seemed admirable." Usage is, primarily, talk; and talk year by year gives words differing social approval, and differing meanings. Words move from the gutter to the penthouse, and back down the elevator shaft. *Bull,* a four-letter Anglo-Saxon word, was unmentionable in Victorian circles. One had to use *he-cow,* if at all. Phrases and syntactical patterns also have their fashions, mostly bad. *Like unto me* changes to *like me* to *like I do; this type of thing* becomes *this type thing; -wise,* after centuries of dormancy in only a few words (*likewise, clockwise, otherwise*), suddenly sprouts out the end of everything: *budgetwise, personalitywise, beautywise, prestigewise.* As usual, the marketplace changes more than your money.

But the written language has always refined the language of the marketplace. The Attic Greek of Plato and Aristotle (as Aristotle's remarks about local usages show) was distilled from commercial exchange. Cicero and Catullus and Horace polished their currency against the archaic and the Greek. Mallarmé claimed that Poe had given "un sens plus pur aux mots de la tribu"—which Eliot rephrases for himself: "To purify the dialect of the tribe." It is the very nature of writing so to do; it is the writer's illusion that he has done so:

> I have laboured to refine our language to grammatical purity, and to clear it from colloquial barbarisms, licentious idioms, and irregular combinations. Something, perhaps, I have added to the elegance of its construction, and something to the harmony of its cadence.

—wrote Samuel Johnson as he closed his *Rambler* papers. And he had almost done what he hoped. He was to shape English writing for the next hundred years, until it was ready for another dip in the stream and another purification. His work, moreover, lasts. We would not imitate it now; but we can read it with pleasure, and imitate its enduring drive for excellence.

Johnson goes on to say that he has "rarely admitted any word not authorized by former writers." This is the second level of usage, the paper money. But even this usage requires principle. If we accept "what the best writers use," we still cannot tell whether it is sound: we may be aping their bad habits. President Kennedy's inaugural address, carefully polished by Harvard's best, contains this oddity (my italics): "For man holds in his mortal hands the power to abolish *all form* of human poverty and *all form* of human life." Clearly, he meant either *all forms* or *every form*— or *all* human poverty and *all* human life. This mixing of choices, this coupling of the collective *all* with singular *form,* can mean only something like "all traces of form," as if the President were melting a statue. Most singular indeed! Even the best go wrong.

So we cannot look to usage for our rules. Usage is only a court of first appeal, when we can say no more than "He did it." Beyond that helpless litigation, we can test our writing by reason, and by simple principles: clarity is good, economy is good, ease is good, gracefulness is good, fullness is good, forcefulness is good. As with all predicaments on earth, we judge by appeal to principles, and we often find principles in conflict. Is it economical but unclear? Is it full but cumbersome? Is it clear but too colloquial for grace? Careful judgment will give the ruling.

Which is right, "I feel *bad*" or "I feel *badly*"? "The dress looks *good* on her" or "The dress looks *well* on her"? The man on the street would say, "I feel *bad*" and "The dress looks *good,*" and he would be right: not because of "usage," but because *badly* would indicate shaky fingers and *well* a dress with good eyes. "Tie it tight" means "Tie it so that it is tight." "Tie it tightly" means "Tie it as if you were drunk." Unfortunately, people trying to be proper follow the pattern of "He writes badly" and fall into the errors of "I feel badly" and "Tie it tightly." But *writes badly* is a verb with an adverb telling how the action is done, and *feel bad* is a verb with a predicate adjective modifying the subject and telling how the subject *is*. The predicate adjective describes existences, as in *ring true* and *come thick:* "they ring, and they are true"; "they come, and they are thick." So it is with other verbs pointing to states of being—*seem, appear, become, grow, sound, smell, taste* —on which "good usage" might rule the wrong way. Just remember that you don't say "I feel goodly." Let reason be your guide.

Likewise with *the reason . . . is because.* You can find this colloquial redundancy on many a distinguished page. But everything a good writer writes is not necessarily good. The phrase is a collision between two choices, as the mind rushes after its meaning: between (1) *the reason is that . . .* and (2) *it is . . . because.* Delete *the reason . . . is,* the colloquial pump-primer, and you save three words, sometimes four (the following eminent sentence, in which I have bracketed the surplus words, also suffers some redundancy of the *be's*):

> In general it may be said that [the reason why] scholasticism was held to be an obstacle to truth [was] because it seemed to discourage further inquiry along experimental lines.

And so, usage is perhaps where we begin; but if we end there, we may end in wordiness and mediocrity.

PRACTICAL PRESCRIPTIONS FOR GOOD WRITING

A/an. Use *a* before *h* sounded in an accented first syllable: *a HOSpital, a HAMburger.* Use *an* before a silent or an unaccented *h: an honor, an hisTORical event, an halLUcination.*

Affect. Don't use it as a noun; just say *feeling* or *emotion. Affective* is jargon for *emotional* or *emotive. Affect* is a verb meaning "to produce an *effect.*"

All right. *Alright* is not all right; you are thinking of *already.*

Also. Do not use for *and,* especially to start a sentence: not "*Also,* it failed," but simply "And it failed."

And/or. Don't write "fish and/or chips"; write "fish or chips, or both."

Anyone. Don't write *any one* unless you mean *any one thing,* or *any body* unless you mean *any corpse.*

Appearing. Don't write "a comfortable appearing house." This means a comfortable house that keeps appearing by magic. "A comfortable looking house" is not much better. Write "a comfortable house" or "the house seemed comfortable."

As. Use where the cigarette people have *like:* "It tastes good, *as* a goodie should." (See also *Like.*)

Do NOT use for *such as:* "Many things, *as* nails, hats, toothpicks . . . ." Write "Many things, *such as* nails . . . ."

And do NOT use for *because* or *since;* it is ambiguous:

Wrong	Right
As I was walking, I had time to think.	*Since* I was walking, I had time to think.

As . . . as. Use positively, not forgetting the second *as:*

Wrong	Right
as long if not longer	*as* long *as* the other, if not longer

Negatively, use *not so . . . as:*

It is *not so* long *as* the other.

Things are *not so* clear or *so* thorough *as* they ought to be.

As if. Takes the subjunctive:

as if he *were* cold

As to. Use only at the beginning of a sentence: "As to his first allegation, I can only say . . . ." Change it to *about,* or omit it, within a sentence. "He knows nothing *about* the details"; "He is not sure [as to] [whether] they are right."

At. Do not use after *where.* "Where is it *at?*" means "Where is it?"

Between, among. *Between* ("by twain") has TWO in mind; *among* has several. You cannot be between him and me and the gatepost. But "between you and I" is worse: see *Me,* below.

But, cannot but. "He can but fail" is old but usable. After a negative, however, the natural turn in *but* causes confusion:

Poor	Improved
He cannot *but* fail.	He can only fail.
He could not doubt *but* that it	He could not doubt that it . . . .
He could not help *but* take	He could not help taking . . . .

Similarly, *but*'s too close or frequent keep your reader spinning:

Poor	Improved
The campaign was successful *but* costly. *But* the victory was sweet.	The campaign was costly, *but* victory was sweet.

Can. Do not use for permission, or possibility: "Can I have?" means "Do I have the physical capacity to have?" Use *may*. In assertions, the distinction is clear: "He can do it." "He may do it." "He may if he can."

Cannot hardly, couldn't hardly. Use *can hardly, could hardly.*

Case. Chop out this deadwood:

Poor	Improved
In many cases, there are	There are often . . . .
In such a case, surgery is recommended.	Then surgery is recommended.
In case he goes	If he goes . . . .
Everyone enjoyed himself, except for a few scattered cases.	Almost everyone enjoyed himself.

Center around. A physical impossibility; you are thinking around a center. Make it: *centers on,* or *concerns,* or *is about.*

Clichés. Don't use them unwittingly. But you *can* use them very effectively if you know what you are about. There are two kinds: (1) the literary—*tried and true, the not too distant future, sadder and wiser, in the style to which she had become accustomed;* (2) the proverbial—*apple of his eye, skin of your teeth, sharp as a tack, quick as a flash, twinkling of an eye.* The literary ones are rhetorical, clinched by sound alone; the proverbial are metaphors caught in the popular fancy.

Used frugally, these proverbial clichés can lighten a dull passage. You may even revitalize them (see p. 71). The literary ones are to be avoided. But you can also take advantage even of them, if they have not taken advantage of you. You can write *tried and untrue, gladder and wiser, a future not too distant.*

Compare. *To compare to* is to show similarities (and differences) between different kinds; to *compare with* is to show difference (and similarities) between like kinds. *Compare and contrast* is redundant.

Composition has been compared *to* architecture.
He compares favorably *with* Mickey Spillane.
Compare Shakespeare *with* Ben Jonson.

Comparisons. Make them complete; add a *than* phrase or clause:

It is more like a jigsaw puzzle *than a rational plan.*
They are more thoughtful *than the others.*
The first is better *than the second.* (Or "The first is *the* better.")

Connected with, in connection with. These expressions usually mean *about, with,* or *in,* and are always wordy:

Poor	*Improved*
They discussed several things connected with history.	They discussed several historical questions.
They liked everything in connection with the university.	They liked everything about the university.
He is connected with the Smith Corporation.	He is with the Smith Corporation.

Consider, consider as. The first means *believe to be;* the second, *think about* or *speak about;* "I consider him excellent." "I consider him first as a student, then as a man."

Contact. Don't *contact* anyone: get in touch with him, call him, write him, find him, tell him. Don't make a good *contact,* make a useful friend.

Continual, continuous. You can improve your writing by *continual* practice, but the effort cannot be *continuous.* The first means "frequently repeated"; the second, "without interruption."

It requires continual practice.

There was a continuous line of clouds.

Couple. Use *two, a few,* or *several.* Only the breeziest occasions will allow *a couple of.*

Curriculum. The plural is *curricula;* the adjective, *curricular.*

The school offers three separate curricula.

Extracurricular activities also count.

Data. A plural, like *curricula, strata, phenomena:*

The data are inconclusive.

Definitely. A high-school favorite. Cut it out.

Different than. Never use the phrase. Things differ *from* each other. Only in comparing differences could *than* be used: "All three of his copies differ from the original, but his last one is *more* different *than* the others." But here *than* is controlled by *more,* not by *different.*

Wrong	*Right*
It is different *than* I expected.	It is different *from* what I expected.
	It is not what I expected.
This is different *than* all the others.	This is different *from* all the others.

Disinterested. Do not use for *uninterested. Disinterested* means impartial, without private interests in the issue.

Wrong	*Right*
You seem disinterested in the case.	You seem uninterested in the case.
	The judge was disinterested and perfectly fair.

Due to. Never begin a sentence with "*Due to* circumstances beyond his control, he . . . ." *Due* is an adjective and must always relate to a noun or pronoun: "The catastrophe *due to* circumstances beyond his control was unavoidable," or "The catastrophe was *due to* circumstances beyond his control" (predicate adjective). But you are still better off with *because of, through, by,* or *owing to.*

Wrong	*Right*
He resigned due to sickness.	He resigned because of sickness.
He succeeded due to hard work.	He succeeded through hard work.
He lost his shirt due to leaving it in the locker room.	He lost his shirt by leaving it in the locker room.
The Far East will continue to worry the West, due to a general social upheaval.	The Far East will continue to worry the West, owing to a general social upheaval.

Effect. As a noun, it means *result;* as a verb, *to bring about* (not to be confused with *to affect,* meaning *to concern, impress, touch, seize upon,* and the like).

What was the effect?
He effected a thorough change.
How did it affect you?

Enormity. Means "atrociousness"; does not mean "enormousness."

The enormity of the crime.
The enormousness of the mountain.

Enthuse. Don't use it:

Wrong	*Right*
She *enthused* over her new dress.	She gushed on and on about her new dress.
He was *enthused.*	He was enthusiastic.

Equally as good. A redundant mixture of two choices, *as good as* and *equally good.* Use only one of these at a time.

Etc. Substitute something specific for it, or drop it, or use something like "and so forth":

Poor	*Improved*
She served fruit, cheese, candies, etc.	She served fruit, cheese, candies, and little sweet pickles.
	She served fruit, cheese, candies, and the like.

Factor.   Avoid it:

Poor	Improved
The increase in female employment is a factor in juvenile delinquency.	The increase in female employment has contributed to juvenile delinquency.
Puritan self-sufficiency was an important factor in the rise of capitalism.	Puritan self-sufficiency favored the rise of capitalism.

Farther, further.   The first means distance; the second means time or figurative distance. You look *farther* and consider *further*.

Firstly.   Archaic. Trim all such terms to *first, second, third,* and so on.

Fix.   The word means *to establish in place;* it means *to repair* only in speech or colloquial writing.

Flaunt, flout.   *Flaunt* means to parade, to wave impudently; *flout* means to scoff at. The first is metaphorical; the second, not: "She *flaunted* her wickedness and *flouted* the police."

Folks.   Use *parents, mother and father,* or *family* instead.

Former and latter.   Passable, but they often make the reader look back. It is better simply to repeat the antecedents.

Poor	Improved
The Athenians and Spartans were always in conflict. *The former* had a better civilization; *the latter* had a better army.	The Athenians and Spartans were always in conflict. Athens had the better culture; Sparta, the better army.

Gray.   America prefers *gray* to *grey* (the British usage).

Hanged, hung.   *Hanged* is the past of *hang* only for the death penalty.

They hung the rope and hanged the man.
The rope was hung; the man was hanged.

However.   Bury it between commas, or replace it with *but* or *nevertheless.*

Poor	Improved
However, the day had not been entirely lost.	*But* the day had not been entirely lost.
However, the script that Alcuin invented became the forerunner of modern handwriting.	The script that Alcuin invented, *however,* became the forerunner of modern handwriting.

Initial *However* should be an adverb:

However long it takes, it will be done.
However she did it, she did it well.

Identify. Give it an object:

He *identified the wallet.*
He *identified himself* with the hero. (*Not* "He identified with the hero.")

Imply, infer. The author *implies;* you *infer* ("carry in") what you think he means.

He *implied* that all women were hypocrites.
From the ending, we *infer* that tragedy ennobles what it kills.

Inside of, outside of. Redundant expressions; avoid them:

Poor	Improved
inside of half an hour	in half an hour
inside of the house	inside the house
He had nothing for dinner outside of a few potato chips.	He had nothing for dinner but a few potato chips.

Instances. Redundant. *In many instances* means *often, frequently.*

Interesting. Make what you say interesting, but never tell the reader *it is interesting:* he may not believe you. *It is interesting* is merely a lazy preamble:

Poor	Improved
It is interesting to note that nicotine is named for Jean Nicot, who introduced tobacco into France in 1560.	Nicotine is named for Jean Nicot, who introduced tobacco into France in 1560.

Irony. Not the same as sarcasm (which see). A clash between appearance and reality. There seem to be three kinds:

Verbal irony. You say the opposite of what you mean: "It's a *great* day," appearing to mean *great* but really meaning *terrible*.

Dramatic irony. Someone unwittingly states the opposite of the truth. A character in a play, for example, might say "This is my great day," when the audience has just seen his daughter abducted and the mortgage foreclosed.

Irony of circumstance. The opposite of what ought to happen happens (it rains on the day of the Weather Bureau's picnic; the best man of all is killed); and we are sharply aware of the contrast.

Irregardless. No such word. The *ir-* (meaning *not*) is doing what the *-less* already does. You are thinking of *irrespective,* and trying to say *regardless.*

Kind of, sort of. Colloquialisms for *somewhat, rather, something,* and the like. "It is *kind of* odd" will not get by. But "It is *a kind of* academic hippopotamus" will get by nicely, because *a kind of* means *a species of.*

Lay. Don't use *lay* to mean *lie. Lay* means *to put* and needs an object; *lie* means *to recline.* Memorize both their present and past tenses, which are frequently confused:

I *lie* down when I can; I *lay* down yesterday; I have *lain* down often.

The hen *lays* an egg; she *laid* one yesterday; she has *laid* four this week.

Now I *lay* the book on the table; I *laid* it there yesterday; I have *laid* it there many times.

Lend, loan. Don't use *loan* for *lend. Lend* is the verb; *loan,* the noun: "Please *lend* me a five; I need a *loan* badly." Remember the line from the song: "I'll *send* you to a *friend* who'll be willing to *lend.*"

Less, few. Do not use one for the other. *Less* answers "How much?" *Few* answers "How many?"

Wrong	*Right*
We had *less* people than last time.	We had *fewer* people this time than last.

Like, as, as if. Learn to distinguish these three. *Like* is a preposition, taking an object; when a verb follows, use *as* or *as if:*

He looks *like* me.
He dresses *as* I do.
He acts *as if* he *were* mad.

Note that *like* takes the objective case, and that *as*, being a conjunction, is followed by the nominative:

She looks like *her.*
He is as tall as *I* [am].
He is tall, like *me.*

The pattern of the prepositional phrase (*like me, like a house, like a river*) has caused *like* to replace *as* where no verb follows in phrases other than comparisons (*as . . . as*):

It works *like* a charm. (*. . . as* a charm *works.*)
It went over *like* a lead balloon. (*. . . as* a lead balloon *does.*)
They worked *like* beavers. (*. . . as* beavers *do.*)

Notice that *as* would give these three statements a meaning of substitution or disguise: "It works as a charm" (but it really isn't a charm); "It went over as a lead balloon" (disguised as a lead balloon).

Manner. Drop this from your working vocabulary. *In a . . . manner* is a favorite redundancy. Replace it with an adverb: *in a clever manner* means *cleverly; in an awkward manner* means *awkwardly.*

Me. Use *me* boldly. It is the proper object of verbs and prepositions. Nothing is sadder than faulty propriety: "between you and *I*," or "They gave it to John and *I*," or "They invited my wife and *I*." Test yourself by dropping the first member: "between *I*" (*no*), "gave it to *I*" (*no*), "invited *I*" (*no*). And do not substitute *myself.*

Most. Do not use *most* to mean *almost.*

Wrong	*Right*
Most everyone knows.	Almost everyone knows.

Myself. Use it only reflexively ("I hurt *myself*"), or intensively ("I *myself* often have trouble"). Fear of *me* leads to the incorrect

"They gave it to John and *myself.*" Do not use *myself, himself, herself, themselves* for *me, him, her, them.*

Nature. Avoid using the word as padding. Do not write *moderate in nature, moderate by nature, of a moderate nature;* write simply *moderate.*

None. This pronoun means *no one* and takes a singular verb, as do *each, every, everyone, nobody,* and other distributives. Another pronoun referring back to any of these must also be singular. Informally (and carelessly), "none of them" often gets the plural verb; but editing carefully, you will change your *are* to *is.*

Wrong	*Right*
None of them *are* perfect.	None of them *is* perfect.
Nobody brought their pens.	Nobody brought his pen.
Everybody thinks *they have* the worst of it.	Everybody thinks *he has* the worst of it.

One. Avoid this common redundancy.

Poor	*Improved*
One of the most effective ways of writing is rewriting.	The best writing is rewriting.
The Ambassadors is one of the most interesting of James's books.	*The Ambassadors* is James at his best.
The meeting was obviously a poor one.	The meeting was obviously poor.

In constructions such as "one of the best that . . ." and "one of the worst who . . . ," the relative pronouns often are mistakenly considered singular. The plural noun of the prepositional phrase (*best, worst*), not the *one,* is the antecedent, and the verb must be plural too:

Wrong	*Right*
one of the best (*players*) who *has* ever swung a bat	one of the best (*players*) who *have* ever swung a bat

Only. Don't put it in too soon; you will say what you do not mean.

Wrong	*Right*
He *only liked* mystery stories.	He liked *only mystery stories.*

Participle for gerund. Avoid this frequent error. Present participles and gerunds look alike; they are different uses of the *-ing* form of the verb. The participle works as an adjective; the gerund as a noun. You want gerunds in the following constructions, and you can get them by changing the misleading noun or pronoun to the possessive case:

Wrong	*Right*
Washington commended *him passing* through the British lines.	Washington commended *his passing* through the British lines.
Do you mind *me staying* late?	Do you mind *my staying* late?
She disliked *Bill smoking*.	She disliked *Bill's smoking*.
We all enjoyed *them singing* songs and *having* a good time.	We all enjoyed *their singing* songs and *having* a good time.

You can catch these errors by asking yourself if you mean that "Washington commended *him*," or that "She disliked *Bill*" (which you do not).

Per. Use *a:* "He worked ten hours *a* day." *Per* tends to be jargon.

Personally. Always superfluous.

Poor	*Improved*
I want to welcome them *personally*.	I want to welcome them [myself].
Personally, I like it.	I like it.

Phase. *Phase* is not *faze* ("daunt"), nor does it mean *aspect* or *part;* it is a stage in a familiar cycle, like that of the moon or the caterpillar.

Plan on. Use *plan to.*

Wrong	*Right*
He planned on going.	He planned to go.

Prejudice. The illiterate are beginning to write "He was *prejudice*." Their readers are outrage.

Proof, evidence. *Proof* results from enough *evidence* to establish a point beyond doubt. Be modest about claiming proof:

Poor	Improved
This *proves* that Fielding was in Bath at the time.	Evidently, Fielding was in Bath at the time.

Proved, proven. *Proved* is the past participle, which may serve as an adjective meaning "successfully tested or demonstrated"; *proven* is an adjective only, and means "tested by time":

Wrong	Right
It has proven true. [past part.]	It has proved true.
A proven theory [past part. as adj.]	A proved theory
The theory was proven. [same]	The theory was proved.
A proved remedy [pure adj.]	A proven remedy

Real. Do not use for *very*. *Real* is an adjective meaning actual:

Wrong	Right
It was *real* good.	It was *very* good.
	It was *really* good.

Reason . . . is because. Knock out *the reason . . . is,* and you will have a good sentence (see p. 86).

[The **reason**] they have difficulty with languages [is] because they have no interest in them.

Regarding, in regard to. Redundant or inaccurate.

Poor	Improved
Regarding the banknote, Jones was perplexed. [Was he *looking* at it?]	Jones was perplexed by the banknote.
He knew nothing *regarding* money.	He knew nothing about money.
She was careful *in regard* to the facts.	She respected the facts.

Respective, respectively. Redundant.

Poor	Improved
The armies retreated to their *respective* trenches.	The armies retreated to their trenches.
Smith and Jones won the first and second prize *respectively.*	Smith won the first prize; Jones, the second.

Round. British for *around.*

Sarcasm. The student's word for irony. Sarcasm intends personal hurt. It may also be ironic, but need not be. "Well, little man, what now?" is pure sarcasm when a dwarf interrupts the class; it is ironic sarcasm when a seven-footer bursts in. See *Irony.*

Shall, will; should, would. Keep *shall* and *should* for *I*, and *will* and *would* for the others. Switch them to express determination: "*I will* go; they *shall* not pass."

Similar to. Use *like:*

Poor	Improved
This is *similar to* that.	This is *like* that.

Slow. GO SLOW is what the street signs and the men on the street all say, but write "go slowly."

So. Should be followed by *that* in describing extent: "It was *so* foggy *that* traffic almost stopped." Avoid its incomplete form, the school girl's intensive—*so nice, so wonderful, so pretty*—though occasionally this is effective.

Split infinitives. Don't use them. They are cliché traps: *to really know, to really like, to better understand.* They are misleaders: *to better . . . , to further . . . , to well . . . , to even . . . . To better know* is to make *know* better; *to even like* is to make *like* even, all of which is nonsense. Indeed, in perverse moments *to eventually go* seems to say that *go* is being "eventuallied." Finally, they are usually redundant: *to really understand* is *to understand.* The quickest cure for split infinitives is to drop the adverb.

Even the splitters do not recommend splitting as a rule. The rule remains DON'T SPLIT; and if you must, learn what you are doing—a little deviltry is better for the soul than ignorance. But I am convinced that you can always mend the split for a gain in grace, and often for a saving of words. You can sometimes change the adverb to an adjective: "to adequately think out solutions" can become "to think out adequate solutions." Or you can drop the adverb—often exuberant—or bring it forward, or move it along:

Poor	Improved
I cannot bring myself to really like the fellow.	I cannot bring myself to like the fellow.
	I cannot bring myself really to like the fellow.
	I really cannot bring myself to like the fellow.

George O. Curme (*English Grammar*, Barnes & Noble, 1947) gives the following examples from eminent splitters, arguing that usage makes them right. But each of them can be improved:

Poor	Improved
I wish the reader to clearly understand this. (Ruskin)	I wish the reader to understand this.
	I wish the reader to understand this clearly.
It would have overburdened the text to there incorporate many details. (Hempl, *Mod. Lang. Notes*)	Details would have overburdened the text.
. . . without permitting himself to actually mention the name. (Arnold)	. . . without permitting himself to mention the name.
. . . of a kind to directly stimulate curiosity. (Pater)	. . . of a kind to stimulate curiosity.
	. . . of a kind to stimulate curiosity directly.
. . . things which few except parents can be expected to really understand. (Oliver Wendell Holmes)	. . . things only parents can understand.
. . . to bravely disbelieve (Browning, *The Ring and the Book*, Cambridge ed., p. 570)	. . . bravely to disbelieve

Browning's line, in fact, would have thumped somewhat less if he had dared bravely to vary his meter and mend his infinitive like this:

> Whence need bravely to disbelieve report

That, which, who. *That* defines and restricts; *which* is explanatory and nonrestrictive; *who* stands for people, and may be restrictive or nonrestrictive. (See pp. 54 and 76.)

> The faucet *that* drips is in the basement.
> The faucet, *which* drips badly, also needs attention.
> Of all the Democrats *who* supported him at first, none was more ardent than Jones.
> Of all the Democrats, *who* supported him at first, none was more ardent than Jones.

They. A loose indefinite pronoun; tighten it:

Poor	Improved
They are all against us, you know.	*Everyone* is against us, you know.
They launch our rockets at Cape Canaveral.	*The United States* launches its rockets from Cape Canaveral.

Do not use *they* with a singular antecedent.

Wrong	Right
Everyone knows *they* should write correctly.	*Everyone* knows *he* should write correctly.
Every one of the students assumes *they* will pass.	*Every one* of the students assumes *he* will pass.

Till, until. Both respectable. Note the spelling. Do not use '*til.*

Too. Do not use *too* as a conjunctive adverb: "Too, it was unjust." It is also poor as an intensive: "They did not do too well" (note the difference in Shakespeare's "not wisely but too well"—he really means it). Use *very;* or, better, use nothing: "They did not do well."

Trite. From Latin *tritus:* worn out. Many words get temporarily worn out and unusable: *emasculated, viable, situation,* **to**

name a few. And many phrases are permanently frayed: see *Cliché*.

Try and. Use *try to*. *To try and do* means *to try and to do*, which is probably not what you want to say.

Type. Banish it, abolish it. If you must use it, use *of:* not *that type* person but *that type OF person*, though even this is really jargon for *that kind of person, a person like that*. The newspapers have succumbed, and we hear of *commando-type forces* for *commando forces*, of a *Castro-type dictator* for *another Castro*. The most accurate translations of *-type* are *-like, -ish, -esque*, and *-ate*, depending on sense and euphony: *Castro-like, Castro-ish, Russianesque, Italianate*. English has many ways of saying it:

Wrong	*Right*
Mondrian's checkerboard-type painting	Mondrian's checkerboard of a painting
	Mondrian's checkerboardish painting
	Mondrian's checkerboard-like painting
French-type dressing	French dressing
Italian-type spaghetti	Italian spaghetti [Be bold!—we neither know nor care whether it's imported]
atomic-type submarine	atomic submarine
She was a Shirley Temple-type girl.	She was like Shirley Temple.
	She was a Shirley Temple.
	She was a Shirley Temple kind of girl.
An apprentice-type situation	apprenticeship
A string-type playpen	A string playpen
A Puck-type person	A Puckish person, a Puck-like person

Unique. Do not use with a comparative. To call something *unique* means that there is nothing in the world like it.

Wrong	*Right*
The more unique the organization	The more nearly unique . . . .
the most unique man I know	the most nearly unique man I know
a very unique personality	a unique personality

Very. Use sparingly; and the same holds for *quite, rather, pretty,* and *little.* I would hate to admit (and don't care to know) how many of these qualifiers I have cut from this text. You can do without them entirely.

Ways. Use *way:* "He went a short *way* into the woods."

While. Use only for time, as in "While I was talking, she smoked constantly."

Wrong	*Right*
While I like her, I don't admire her.	*Although* I like her, I don't admire her.
The side roads were impassable, *while* the highways were clear.	The side roads were impassable, *but* the highways were clear.
The seniors eat in clubs, *while* the freshmen eat in their dormitories.	The seniors eat in clubs, *and* the freshmen eat in their dormitories.

Whom. The objective form, used after verbs and prepositions; but it is often wrongly used as the subject of a clause.

Wrong	*Right*
Give the ticket to *whomever* wants it.	Give the ticket to *whoever wants it.* [The whole clause is the object of *to.*]
The president, *whom* he said would be late	The president, *who* he said *would be late* . . . . [Commas around *he said* would clear the confusion.]

BUT:

They did not know whom to elect. [The infinitive takes the objective case.]

-wise. Avoid all confections like *marketwise, customerwise, pricewise, gradewise, confectionwise.*

Would. For habitual acts the simple past is more economical:

Poor	Improved
The parliament *would meet* only when called by the king.	The parliament *met* only when called by the king.
Every hour, the watchman *would make* his round.	Every hour, the watchman *made* his round.

Would sometimes seeps into the premise of a supposition. Rule: Don't use *would* in an *if*-clause.

Wrong	Right
If he *would have* gone, he would have succeeded.	If he *had* gone, he would have succeeded.
	Had he gone, he would have succeeded [more economical].
I wish I *would have* learned it.	I wish I *had* learned it.

8 / Three Excursions

THE SEMESTER is now perhaps half over. Very likely you have been writing an essay a week, with exercises in between. You and your instructor are running out of ideas. Now is the time for greener pastures, before the harvest of the research paper. I propose three vacations without leaving the expository area. Each will tone up different linguistic muscles.

THE AUTOBIOGRAPHICAL ESSAY

The problem in this autobiographical excursion will be two-fold: first, to demonstrate a point; second, to describe accurately and vividly a personal experience. You will find yourself writing metaphorically as you try to bring to the reader exactly what your adventure was like. The aim of the exercise is to refresh your language with a dip into the descriptive, that stream of specific sights, sounds, feelings, and figurative comparisons into which regular expository writing rarely ventures.

You will be telling an anecdote. It must be interesting, and anecdotes are interesting only when they demonstrate some old truth about existence, when they offer an example of "they'll do it every time," sharpened to philosophical precision. Your tale may be comic or tragic. Look for the kind you would tell about yourself, or *on* yourself, to the young lady on your right at dinner. It must have a point, or her smile will be thin. For your essay, *cherchez la pointe.*

Suppose this is your proposition: "Pride goeth before a fall."

You have in mind the time you were skating—capering and swooping for admiration, farther and farther, till the ice broke. With no thought at all, you would have known it for a good offering in conversation. In using it for your essay you need more thought, more clarity, and more structure. You need your thesis; you need a beginning, a middle, and an end.

As always, devise your thesis first: "The old saying about pride inviting a fall can prove disastrously true." Now, as always, crank back for your opening sentence. Keep *yourself* out of the beginning paragraph, at least until just before the thesis. You are not really writing about yourself. You are writing an essay about something generally true: you will be illustrating the general proposition with a personal experience, but the general truth is your point. Your beginning paragraph might look like this:

> No one believes that his parents know much. We are all sure that we know better, that all the old warnings are plots to curtail enjoyment, that all old sayings are relics of the Puritans. Furthermore, the parental warning seems a gross underestimation of our powers and maturity. We are insulted; we have been treated as children. Perhaps most of the youthful catastrophes in the evening paper have resulted from illusions of manhood, and resentful pride. This seems to be the way we are made, and all of us are lucky if we escape bodily harm from our own arrogance. The old saying about pride going before a fall can prove disastrously true.

Now for the middle. This tells the story. Your entire episode comes in to illustrate your thesis:

> I learned this one sunny winter afternoon. Five of us, close friends since first grade, had eaten lunch at my house, three blocks from the Willawee River. We had been obstreperous. My mother had been harried and amused as she made more sandwiches, more hot chocolate, and scraped out the last of the pudding. "Now, be careful," she had said as we started to get our things together on the porch. "Now, be careful," I mimicked to the others, feeling too good for thought. She called me into the hall and dressed me down, ending with "Just remember that pride goes before a fall." How I hated that old saying. My grandmother always managed to work it in at least once a visit. As I turned to go, my mother added in a completely different tone: "Please don't go out too far, John. Remember the Simmons boy."

I remembered nothing as I walked away with my grinning companions—except my resentment, a small dull twist in my stomach even after the bright afternoon had lifted all of us again to our lunchtime heights. The air was like alcohol on the skin. Everything sparkled in the clear air; everything seemed closer than normal. The river looked like frosting, but down the middle a dull green vein straggled.

And so, on to the climax, which now threatens to be tragic. You, of course, would know, because your experience, unlike the one above, would have been real.

The value of the exercise depends on its being real. This puts a demand on your powers different from that of logical progressions. This asks you not to think up a subject and think out its consequences, but to render as truly and particularly as possible a subject already there, something you have experienced but have perhaps never put into words, never fully conveyed to someone else. It asks you to fill out the half-remembered circumstances into a picture very like what they were, a picture that will let others see how it was. You could tell the whole thing in three sentences: "I dared Bill to follow. We fell in. He froze and drowned." But you need to do what every storyteller must do: keep from telling the story, keep it from ending, without losing your reader's patience. You need detail and detail and detail, simile after simile after metaphor, to postpone the climax and to let us see and feel how it was.

The ending may be no more than a sentence, or it may be a ruminative paragraph, generalizing upward and outward from the particulars to mirror the beginning paragraph, as in a regular essay. The dramatic curve of your incident will tell you what to do. It may be well to end when the story has told itself out, and made its point starkly: "The four of us walked numbly up the street toward home."

THE TERRIBLE ESSAY

Now that you have had an excursion into figurative language, and have seen what concrete words can do, you will go on a treasure hunt for the horrendously abstract. Nothing can be more salutary. You will work out all the fever. Again we follow the essay form, this time in parody not only of the form itself, but especially of that abstract lint the bad essay uses for language. You write the worst essay you can think of.

First, some rules:

1. Use no other verb but *is*. Rule 2, then, will be easy.
2. Put EVERYTHING in the passive voice.
3. Use no adjectives; use nouns instead. An *excellent idea* becomes *the conception of an excellence program*. Do not say *governmental spending*; say *government spending*.
4. Use no participles; use verbs with *which*: not *dripping*, but *which drip*.
5. Use only one adverb for everything, and pick a good big cloudy one like *considerably* or *indubitably*—nothing like *sharply*, or *painfully*, or *crazily*, or *happily*.
6. Use only big abstract nouns—as many *-tion*'s as possible.
7. Use plenty of *of*'s and *which*'s.
8. Use as many words as possible to say the least. Say "It has been considerably in evidence for a considerable period of time that something is in a state of putrefaction in one of the most time-honored and revered of Nordic commonwealths and principalities" instead of "Something is rotten in the state of Denmark" (even Shakespeare could use a few words too many).
9. Work in as many trite expressions as possible: *Needless to say, all things being equal, in the foreseeable future, a better world in which to live.*
10. Sprinkle heavily with *-wise*-type and *type*-type expressions.
11. Compile a basic vocabulary: *situation, aspect, function, factor, phase, -type, -wise*—the class may well cooperate in this.

As with all rules, you can sometimes break these to good effect. Were you to follow them meticulously you would be unintelligible. What you want is a parody of badness, with enough goodness to make it fun. Your project will be an ultra-serious study of trivia. I propose: *A Report of a Study of the Person Sociology and Night Loss Cost Economics of the Faucets Which Drip in the Second Floor North Corner Woman Dormitory Lavatory.*

Now write a good bad beginning paragraph:

The necessity of cleanliness is considerably in evidence to everyone who is concerned in the creation of a better world in which to live. Water is necessary to be utilized by every life thing.

It will not be denied that young women of the college-type category should not be excluded from consideration in this connection. As a consequence of this nature-life principle, which is a major aspect of the situation, every dormitory on the property of the campus of the University of Blank has been provided with a number of examples of lavatories of a tile-chromium nature. They have the appearance of being adequate, and of being the result of an investment utility program of an economy-necessity nature. However, careful investigation of the science objective type has disclosed a large number of factors phasewise, the chief of which is that a number of chromium fixture lavatory faucets function in a manner not in accordance with economy or utility. All things being equal, they drip. The present study is an examination of the lavatation of a representative example, with conclusion in regard to confusion between a water waste compulsion type individual and a drip.

With ingenuity you can keep this going throughout your essay, filling out a sober middle with statistics and an elegant end with pomp.

THE IRONIC ESSAY

Your Terrible Essay has, of course, been ironic. In it, you have feigned an appearance contrary to reality. To spoof the errors of earnest professionalism, you have pretended to be an earnest professional. You have practiced one kind of verbal irony, making your words mean the opposite of what they say. They have appeared to say "This is serious and important"; they have really said that all of it—with the whole mode of vanity it represents—is nonsense. You have proceeded, furthermore, with a perfect understanding that your reader sees the pose and is enjoying it with you.

The first requirement for irony, then, is an understanding shared between author and reader. It is like Pig Latin, or any other secret language, in which two can talk and circumvent a third. It is, in William Empson's words, a way of getting by the censor. The pleasure in irony is the smuggler's pleasure. I can say, "It was a fine day," and the uninitiated will think it really was; but you and I will know that it was not. The pleasure in the secret, furthermore, gives the truth an emphasis beyond that of bald statement. Alongside irony, plain statement seems uncouth. "It was a terrible day" seems young and petulant; "it was a fine day" is the voice of refined experience, a suggestion of tweed and teacups, Tobruk to El Alamein, tigers in Bengal, and never a hair turned. A few of the guests might think the day's shooting had been good, but the speaker and you and I would know—and enjoy the imperturbed secret, even secretly enjoy the disappointment because it has made irony possible—that the day had been terrible.

For your Ironic Essay, therefore, pick something that is common knowledge. The ironist does not write to one alone, but he writes to all his readers as if each were the only one, complimenting each on his perspicuity. If his subject is not generally and publicly important, he will be talking in riddles. He takes something of public interest—a proposal to raise taxes, for instance. He pretends to be pompous and nearsighted, as if he narrowly misconceives the issue and cannot see the full implications of his words. His pose will be much like yours in the Terrible Essay. He makes his pose the opposite of his true standpoint, at the same time making his true standpoint clear. He writes:

> The popular clamor against the proposed raise in taxes is as shortsighted as it is unfounded. Purging the purse is good for the spleen. What does it matter that the present Drain Commissioner has wasted exactly a half-million dollars on a poorly conceived plan? What does it matter that our fine city council now finds it necessary to ask for a new bond and a new assessment to overhaul a drainage system just four years old? It matters not. The moral discipline of digging deeper into the pocket so that the Commissioner may dig a deeper drain is good for the soul, even if we must all skip a meal now and then and take out a second mortgage. There is nothing like good drainage.

Or he writes:

> The public has again expressed its infinite wisdom in voting down the recent bond issue. Niggardliness is next to godliness, as my great-uncle used to say. It really does not matter that classrooms built for twenty are desperately trying to hold forty; nor that our best teachers are leaving for Southfield and Adams and Middlebranch, and even Potfield, simply because they can no longer teach the numbers of students pouring into our beautiful

Smith School—one of our most revered landmarks, by the way, and certainly the oldest. If we can save enough for our beer and T.V. tubes, our children's education really does not matter. We're keeping them off the streets, aren't we?

This mixing of fact and irony exacts careful wording. The two examples above seek to keep clear the line between straight statement and ironic inversion. It does matter, the writer implies, that the local classrooms are crowded. It is true that they are crowded to almost twice their effective capacity; it is true that at least three good teachers have left for positions in Southfield, Adams, and Middlebranch, and that a fourth has even been lured away to dumpy Potfield. The writer calls the public wise and means foolish; yet he calls them niggardly and means niggardly. How does he do it?

The first clue is overstatement: *expressed its infinite wisdom* is a rotund circumlocution for *wise,* and *infinite wisdom* is a cliché. Then the language goes straight, and we know that the bond issue was, in fact, defeated. The tactics change in the next sentence. Here the writer calls a spade a spade but uses it as an argument for the opposition, making it a poor argument by the harshness of *niggardliness* and the absurdity of its new setting in the old proverb. He implies that the opposing arguments are just that poorly founded. The next sentence makes its irony clear when the facts of two-for-one crowding controvert the opening phrase, making it pure verbal irony: *it does not matter* means *it does matter.* And so on. *Beautiful* means *ugly;* the building is old and it is a landmark, all right, but if it is revered it is wrongly revered.

Now, the writer did not (as I think I can testify) ask himself "Is this an overstatement?" or "Is this an understatement?" or "Is this a cliché?" He simply had his point in mind, took the ironic stance, and struck the ironic tone. He allowed his language to inflate itself, or to drop below the line (*it really does not matter*) as he went along, assuming the ironic pose, the ignorant pose, and dropping it when he wanted to go straight. He knows that his audience is with him, or that the secret appeal of irony will make them wish they were.

Your first step is to take some current campus issue, in which you will have a supporting audience. A topic that has worked well in its simplicity and perennial currency is the state of dormitory food. Actually, dormitory food is not bad, but then it is not what mother used to make either. You can probably think of enough amusing detail to make you glad of the opportunity for irony its mediocrity affords. So: your real thesis is that dormitory food is horrible. Your ironic thesis, obviously, will be: "Dormitory food is absolutely delicious." Now, put on the blinkers; narrow your vision down to that one point. You cannot possibly understand how anyone can complain of such a splendid cuisine. Your first paragraph will go something like this:

THE DELICACIES OF THE SMITH HALL STEAMTABLE

It is one of man's perversities to complain. Give him a new suit, and he complains that his neckties do not match. Give him a new car, and he complains about the size of his garage. Give a child what is good for him and he complains that he does not like it. Food, in fact, is one of man's oldest complaints. Adam and Eve got tired of the bill of fare even in Paradise, and there is no better roughage in the world than fruit and raw vegetables. It is the same old story in Smith Hall. Give students paradise and they want steak. Give them steak even as frequently as once a year, and they complain that it is thin or cold or dried out. The diet at the Smith Hall steamtable, as any educated palate can tell, is delicious; and though to a handful of irascible latecomers it may seem cold and dry and unappetizing, it is nonetheless extremely well balanced: in fact, it never changes.

Now, if you wish, take this as your beginning paragraph, adjust it to your needs, and write on—through the delights of cold mashed potatoes, plastic whipped cream, and gravied bus boys, not forgetting to fashion a rich and impassioned peroration as your end paragraph. Any other convenient local topic will do. The trick is to find the ironic stance and tone, and through irony to learn the weights of words.

SUGGESTIONS FOR TOPICS

1. *The Autobiographical Essay:* an automobile accident, a harrowing experience as camp counselor, a family picnic, a party that flopped, a new friend who clung, a disappointing trip, a first week at college
2. *The Terrible Essay:* book-borrowers, lawnsitters, the habits of

smokers, the way professors enter the classroom, library daydreamers, fashions in lipstick, creaking doors

3. *The Ironic Essay:* the joys of learning languages by tape, Chinese made easy, happy college days, the beloved roommate, the eight o'clock class, our courteous age, chivalry is not dead, the joy of cooking, college—the home away from home

9 / The Research Paper

Now to consolidate and advance. Instead of one thousand words you will write three thousand. Instead of a self-propelled debate you will write a scholarly argument. You will also learn to use the library, and to take notes and give footnotes. You will learn the manners of scholarship. You will learn to acknowledge your predecessors as you distinguish yourself, to make not only a bibliography, but a contribution.

The research paper is very likely not what you think it is. *Re*-search is searching again. You are looking, usually, where others have looked before; but your aim is to see something they have not seen. Research is not combining a paragraph from *The Encyclopaedia Britannica* and a paragraph from *The Book of Knowledge* with a slick pinch from *Life*. That's robbery. Nor is it research if you carefully change each phrase and acknowledge the source. That's drudgery. Even in some high circles, I am afraid, such scavenging is called research. It is not. It is simply a cloudier condensation of what you have done in school as a "report"— sanctioned plagiarism to teach something about ants or Ankara, a tedious compiling of what is already known. That such material is new to you is not the issue: it is already in the public stock.

Choosing Your Subject

Find a thesis. What, then, can you do, with things so well stocked? You move from facts to ideas. Here the range is infinite.

Every old idea needs new assertion. Every new assertion needs judgment. Here you are in the area of value, and of values, where everyone is in favor of virtue but in doubt as to what is virtuous. Your research problem is to make a judgment of right or wrong on some controversial issue.

I have put it bluntly to save you from drowning in slips of paper. Remember that an opinion is not a private fancy; it is an opinion of what the right is, of what the truth is, of what the facts mean. It is a judgment of what *is*—out there someplace, not merely in somebody's head. An opinion, when careful and informed, is as close as anyone will ever get to truth: a statement of what the truth of the matter seems to be. Your opinion may be just as accurate as anybody's, and the major task of the research paper is to sift opinions.

Your sifter, as always, is your thesis, right there at the neck of your beginning paragraph—which, as always, is your essay in miniature. Make your thesis first, *before you begin researching*. Call it an hypothesis (a "sub-thesis") if that will make you comfortable. It does seem unscientific. But it is nearer the scientific method than it looks. The scientist, too, plays his hunches. James Watt saw the steam condenser in the lid of his aunt's teakettle; Donald Glaser saw the tracks of atomic particles in the bubbles of his beer. As with scientific experiment and the simple essay, if the hypothesis proves wrong the testing will have furnished means to make it more nearly right. With the research paper, if you do not have a thesis to lead you through the twists and turns of print, you will never come out the other end. Unless you have a working hypothesis to keep your purpose alive as you collect, you may collect forever, forever hoping for a purpose. If you have a thesis, you will learn—and then overcome—the temptations of collecting only the supporting evidence and ignoring the obverse facts and whispers of conscience. If further facts and good arguments persuade you to the other side, so much the better. You will be the stronger for it.

Persuade your reader you are right. You do not search primarily for facts. You do not aim to summarize everything ever said on the subject. You aim to persuade your reader that the thesis you believe in is right. You persuade him by: (1) letting him see that you have been thoroughly around the subject and that you know what is known of it and thought of it, (2) showing him where the wrongs are wrong, and (3) citing the rights as right. *Your opinion, your* thesis, is what you are showing; all your quotations from all the authorities in the world are subservient to *your* demonstration. You are the reigning authority: you have, for the moment, the longest perspective and the last word.

Pick an argument. The tactics of the research paper, then, are exactly those of any argumentative essay. Of course, you can give even straight exposition an argumentative edge: you can take as a subject not just "House Cats" but "House cats are more intelligent than most people realize." You can find something to prove even in straight description: "See," you say, "this has been overlooked; this has not been appreciated; this has been misunderstood." But you will be stronger yet in dealing with a controversial topic. Therefore: (1) pick a subject in which there is much to be said on both sides; (2) take the side where your heart is; (3) write a thesis sentence with a *because* in it; (4) gather your material around and about the *pro* and *con;* (5) write an essay with beginning, middle, and end, and with a *pro*-and-*con* structure like one of those described on pages 11–13.

Pick something that interests you. You need not shake the world. Such subjects as "Subsidized College Football," "Small College Versus Big University," or the worth of "A Best-Selling Novel" well suit the research paper—a three-fold elaboration of the simple essay involving: (1) the handling of your argument, (2) the citation of others' facts and arguments *as part of your own,* and (3) the managing of footnotes and bibliography. Bigger subjects, of course, will try your mettle: subjects like "The Rights of Slaveholders in the Old South," "Euthanasia," "Socialized Medicine." The whole question of governmental versus private endeavors affords many lively issues for research and decision—the ills and virtues of commercial television, for instance.

THE PROCEDURES OF RESEARCH

Get the equipment, and gather the material. First, some 3 x 5 cards for your bibliography, some 3 x 5 slips of paper for notes, and some kind of envelope to hold them. Since you will work up your bibliography first, you may find that your cards still have enough room on face and back for whatever notes you need. Since notes should be brief and few, the limits of your one bibliographical card per source may keep you trim. If you take several notes from each source, however, use your slips of paper and put only one note, even if only a phrase, on each slip. This will facilitate your shuffling and organizing. Plan on some ten or twenty sources for your 3,000 words of text. Make all entries, take all notes, in *ink*. After the thumbing, you will be thankful. You will fill out your cards as you find what you want in card catalogues and indexes. Italicize (that is, underline) titles of books and magazines; put titles of articles found *within* books and magazines in quotation marks. Your cards will look something like this:

BOOK

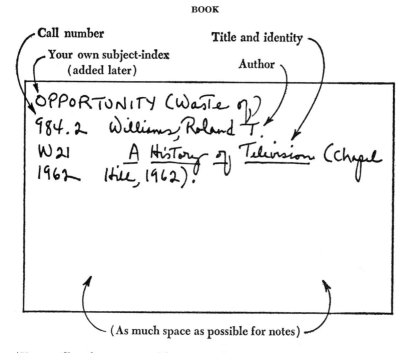

(You will, of course, add your subject-heading only after you have had a look at the book and found it useful.)

ARTICLE

COSTS
AP3
A4
(undergrad.
Stacks)

Johnson, Paul Jr.
"Three Thousand a Minute,"
American Nation, XVI (June
1953), 319–333.

(This is old enough to be bound and in the stacks—hence the call number.)

NEWS STORY

CONTROL
AN
23
.N5
N595

"Commission Recommends T.V.
Control," New York Times, Jan. 6,
1955, Sec. 1, p. 4.

You will check spellings, volume numbers, places, dates, and pages, when you finally get your magazine or book in hand, putting a light √ in pencil to assure yourself that your card is authoritative, safe to use in checking your finished paper. Get the author's name as he signed it, adding detail in brackets if helpful: D[elmar] P[rince] Smith. Get all the information; the sample footnotes on pages 126 through 128 will show you what you may need, especially in complicated references.

Start with encyclopedias. Find *The Encyclopaedia Britannica*, the card catalogue, and the *Reader's Guide to Periodical Literature*, and your problems are nearly solved. Begin with the *Britannica*. This will survey your subject (unless it is something like the latest news from Africa) and will refer you at the end to several authorities. If someone's initials appear at the end, look them up in the list just after the title page in each volume: the author is an authority himself, and you should mention him in your paper. The Index (the last volume in the set) will also refer you to data scattered through all the volumes. Under "Medicine," for instance, the Index directs you to such topics as "Academies," "Hypnotism," "Licensing," "Mythology," "Sanskrit works," and "Women practitioners." Since the University of Chicago now revises the *Britannica* (14th ed.) volume by volume, look at the date on the title page to see by how much you may need to bring your subject up to date. *The Encyclopedia Americana,* though less celebrated, will counteract the Anglocentricity of the *Britannica*. Others will help:

The American Yearbook
Catholic Encyclopedia
Cyclopedia of American Agriculture
Cyclopedia of American Government
Cyclopedia of Education
Commerce Yearbook
Dictionary of American Biography [abbreviated *DAB* in footnotes]
Dictionary of American History
Dictionary of the Bible
Dictionary of National Biography [British—abbreviated *DNB* in footnotes]
Dictionary of Philosophy and Psychology
Encyclopedia of Banking and Finance

Encyclopedia of Religion and Ethics
Encyclopedia of Social Sciences
Encyclopedia of World History
Grove's Dictionary of Music and Musicians
Harper's Encyclopedia of Art
Hutchinson's Technical and Scientific Encyclopedia
Jewish Encyclopedia
The Statesman's Yearbook
Who's Who [British]
Who's Who in America

The World Almanac and Book of Facts, a paperbacked mine of news and statistics (issued yearly since 1868), can provide a factual nugget for almost any subject.

Comb the indexes. With your encyclopedic background sketched, go next to the card catalogue, then to the magazine indexes. Both use the same system, listing each work three times (alphabetically): by author, by title, and by subject. Izaak Walton's *Compleat Angler* would be listed under "Walton, Izaak" and under "*Compleat Angler*" and again under "Fishing," and a good index would also include "Angling—see Fishing." The index directs you around within itself rather well. So, for your research paper, simply take your subject and see what books your library lists under it. Two or three of the most recent books will probably give you all you want, because each of these, in turn, will refer you, by footnote and bibliography, to important previous works. Make your bibliographical cards as you go.

Now for the *Reader's Guide*—an index of articles (and portraits and poems) in more than two hundred magazines. Again, take the most recent issue, look up your subject, and make out your cards—spelling out the abbreviations of titles and dates according to the key just inside the cover. If you don't spell them out fully, your cards may be mysteries to you when you sit down to write. You can drop back a few issues and years to collect more articles; and if your subject belongs to the recent past (after 1907), you can drop back to the right year and track your subject forward.

You can do the same with *The New York Times Index,* beginning with 1914. It will probably lead you to news that appeared in any paper. *The International Index to Periodicals* does for the scholarly journals what the *Reader's Guide* does for the popular ones. Add to these the *Book Review Digest* and the *Biography Index* (which nicely collects scattered references), and you will probably need no more. But here are some others:

Agricultural Index
Annual Magazine Subject-Index [particularly for history]
Art Index
Dramatic Index
Education Index
Essay and General Literature Index [very useful for locating particular subjects within collections of essays]
Industrial Arts Index [for business and technical subjects]
International Catalogue of Scientific Literature
Poole's Index to Periodical Literature (1802–1906)
Portrait Index
Public Affairs Information Service [valuable for "current events" beginning with 1915]
Writings on American History

If you need more, consult Constance M. Winchell's *Guide to Reference Books.*

Take few notes. Now, first the books, then the magazines. With cards in hand, begin with a likely-looking book. Read quickly, with an eye for the general idea, and the telling point. Having a clear thesis will guide your note-taking. You can be sparing and spare. Some of your sources will need notes no fuller than "Violently opposed; recommends complete abolition." This violent and undistinguished author will appear in your paper only among several others in a single footnote to one sentence: "Opposition, of course, has been long and emphatic.²" Now is the time, too, to put a *pro* or a *con* in the upper right corner of your card.

Your next source, however, turns out to have something substantial to say, though still in opposition. This man writes well enough to be quoted. A *con* will put him in his place; a summary phrase will cover him: "Bases argument entirely on practical grounds, sets moral issue aside as irrelevant and 'Utopian.'" Now, within exaggerated quotation marks, put down the sentence or two you want. Your card would look like this:

TAXATION - Private Property   CON
+20.6   Adamson, Charles C.
AM 40   "How Much Can the Traffic Bear?"
          American Investigator, XVI (1920), 210-219.
Bases argument entirely on practical grounds.
Moral issues "Utopian." (210)
"Morals in tax questions are always tied to purse
strings. Where the haves [214] and have-nots haggle,
only practical questions can yield practical
answers...." (213-214) [But couldn't the
moral issues be there anyway? Justice?]

Take care with page numbers. Notice how I have put "214" where the quotation turns the page—I might want to use only part of the excerpt and then be uncertain as to which of the two pages held it. Notice also how I have used brackets around my own words, just to make sure that I don't later confuse them with quoted material. Check your quotation against the original, word for word, and give it a penciled check when you know it is accurate.

Use your slips of paper only if you feel you need more notes than these. Put a "2" in the upper right corner of your first slip; copy and summarize away, using brackets and big quotation marks and putting page numbers in parentheses right where they belong. At the bottom of the slip note the author and page numbers ("Adamson, 215–17"), and start slip 3, if you must. When all your notes are taken, you are ready to write.

THE FIRST DRAFT

Start to plan your paper by writing a beginning paragraph. Formal outlines take more time than they are worth, but a long paper with notes demands some planning. First, draft a beginning paragraph, incorporating your thesis:

THE CASE FOR SOCIALIZED TELEVISION

Freedom for all is the essential idea in a democracy; and free enterprise, it is often said, has made America strong. From the first we have resisted governmental controls, throwing tea into Boston harbor and overthrowing British rule. To this day, "Big Government" usually spells "bad government" to most people, suggesting dictators, inhuman regimentation and terror, and societies of robots. Freedom for the individual is our belief and our goal. But the idea also involves freedom of opportunity, and here, I think, "Big Government" can function, as it has functioned in the past, to prevent one man's enterprise from seizing another man's opportunity. Some such seizure has taken place in the television enterprises of the United States. A brief comparison with the British system, and a little thought, will show that the United States Government could control television with no real damage to free enterprise and with a great widening of opportunity for all. American television is not living up to its opportunities.

Now canvass your notes and plot your course. Read them through, sorting them into three piles: *pro's, con's,* and *in-between's* (often simply facts). Now, by way of outline, make three or four general headings on a sheet of paper, with ample space between. Let us assume a complex *pro*-and-*con* structure. Under each of your headings, make a list of the *con's* against a list of your *pro's*, as they seem to mount and to balance each other. Start with a list of insignificant *con's*, to be finished in a sentence, and move to the more significant. Your sketch will look something like this:

I. Commercial argument—Gov't would still leave room for advertising

Pro	*Con*
	Allenberg
	Hawkings, Weiss
	Smith
	Dillon
	Jones (p. 20)
But—Jones (p. 23)	
Lecky's facts	
N.Y. Times	
Cummings	

II. Educational argument (as against "Entertainment")

    Pro   *Con*

              Perkins

But—Brown (hrs./day
     children watch)

      ⎧ Johnson
Facts   ⎨ Flemming
      ⎪ Steinberg
      ⎩ Lane

III. Freedom to choose—Collins, Williams, Thos. Jefferson "aristocracy of talent."

IV. Opportunity to learn and to be amused—Wilkins.

Notice, first, that your references are thick at first and thin toward the end. As I have said, you will handle each of the first four or five *con*'s in a sentence or two; the rest will get more space. But with Perkins's protests you will leave the *con* side altogether, well before you are halfway through. You will still be citing and quoting under heading III, but these men will all be on your side; and in section IV you will be entirely on your own, except for one stirring quotation from Wilkins.

Put in your references as you go. Your first draft should have all your footnotes, abbreviated, right in the text. Otherwise you will lose your place, and go mad with numbers. Put the notes at the *end* of the last pertinent sentence, with as many of your references as possible grouped in one note. Make your quotations in full, and include the author's surname and the page number with each citation. You will change these in your final draft, of course, filling in the names or leaving them out of the note altogether if they appear in the text. But it will help you in checking against your cards to have an author's name and a page number for each citation. *Don't number your footnotes yet.* When your draft is finished, add the numbers in pencil, so you can change them; circled in red, so you can see them (a red pencil is really worth its price). As you type along, mark your notes with triple parentheses: (((. . .)))— the easiest distinction you can make. Check the rules about quotation marks on pages 57 and 58 (you should single-space and indent all *long* quotations). Now, settle down to the keyboard and begin your second paragraph.

Free enterprise and freedom of opportunity, of course, are the first appeals of those who defend American television as it now is. Any mention of governmental control, or even of change in the present system, is likely to be met with cries of "Socialism" and lectures on the American heritage.[1] (((Allenberg, p. 10; Hawkins, p. 16; Weiss, p. 5; Smith, "This is creeping socialism. This is not the American way," p. 77))) Miles W. Dillon argues that the television networks must awake to their national responsibility in keeping America free by "cleaning their own house" and thus avoiding the governmental intrusion that will be a first step toward absolute governmental control, propaganda, and dictatorship.[2] (((Dillon, pp. 23–25))) Bingham Jones, a proponent of mild governmental regulation, acknowledges these same dangers and concedes that the best solution would be a general renovation by the networks themselves.[3] (((Jones, p. 20)))

But, Jones continues, the networks will never do it; the sponsors are too firmly entrenched:

> If the general housecleaning, so frequently recommended, so frequently attempted, could work, the entire problem would disappear. Our television systems would have arrested their slow deterioration. The lost adult audiences would have been regained . . . . We could again see great works of literature dramatized frequently; we could again explore the world with the informed camera and explore ideas with the best minds of the country. But so long as advertising agents select programs with sales their sole consideration, no house will be cleaned. Indeed, up to the present, every effort at housecleaning has failed after a few preliminary sweeps. Commerce dictates as strongly as ever. (p. 23)

Hans J. Lecky's survey in *T.V. News* indicates that Jones is correct. More than thirty per cent of all television time, Lecky calculates, is given to advertisement. Of the 1000 hours in Lecky's sample, only 50 were "live."[4] (((Lecky, pp. 93–94))) There is some indication, furthermore, that the decline in "live" hours of commercial television has been directly proportional to the decline in quality.[5] (((*Times*, p. 8)))

And so on, until your carded sources run out and your own resources take over completely.

YOUR FINAL DRAFT: DOCUMENTING YOUR SOURCES

Allow space for notes at the foot of the page. You can see from your preliminary drafts about how many footnotes will fall on your page, and about how much space to allow at the bottom. Allow plenty. You will begin your notes three spaces below your text. You have been double-spacing your text; now use a triple-space. Do *not* type a line between text and notes: this indicates a footnote continued from the preceding page. Single-space each note, but double-space between notes. Indent as for a paragraph. Type your number. Press the button at the end of your roller, and roll down about half the height of a capital letter. Begin typing your note without hitting the space bar: " [1] Albert Kurtz, p. 5." After the first line, notes run out to the margin, as in paragraphs. The notes to our sample would come out like this:

> [1] Donald Allenberg, *The Future of Television* (New York, 1958), p. 10; A. H. Hawkins, "Our Greatest Salesman," *American Thought*, IV (1951), 16; J. Weiss, "Government Control, a Growing Concern," *Saturday Night Journal*, September 20, 1958, p. 5; see especially W. W. Smith, "Television and the Modern World," *American Politician*, XIX (1961), 77: "This is creeping socialism. This is not the American way."

> [2] "American Television and Responsibility," *Space*, August 16, 1957, pp. 23–25.

> [3] "Television and Vision: The Case for Governmental Control," *Independent Review*, VIII (1959), 20.

> [4] "A Survey of Programming," May 10, 1960, pp. 93–94.

> [5] "The Trouble with Television" (editorial), New York *Times*, April 10, 1962, Sec. 4, p. 8.

[Notice the comma here: omitted after "Television" and moved behind the parenthesis. Do the same with any parenthetical explanation of a title.]

Footnotes carry only what does not appear in the text. In note 4, for example, only the title of the article, the date, and the pages appear, since the text gives the author and publication. Put as much in the text as possible, without cluttering it. You may have noticed that our long quotation from Jones carried "(p. 23)" at the end, without dropping down to a footnote, and that we needed no title, publication, nor date because we had already given them. Use parentheses like this, even in your own sentences, once you have cited a source (notice where the periods and the quotation marks go):

> Jones further states that advertisers control hiring and firing (p. 24).
>
> Jones further states that "advertisers actually control hiring and firing, one way or another" (p. 24).

Punctuate your footnotes meticulously. The first three entries under our footnote 1 illustrate the three principal kinds of references:

BOOK

Donald Allenberg, *The Future of Television* (New York, 1958), p. 10.

QUARTERLY MAGAZINE

A. H. Hawkins, "Our Greatest Salesman," *American Thought,* **IV** (1951), 16. [Use volume number.]

POPULAR MAGAZINE

J. Weiss, "Government Control, a Growing Concern," *Saturday Night Journal,* September 20, 1958, p. 5. [Ignore volume number, if any.]

As in this last example, give the full date for a popular magazine, instead of Roman numerals and year, and *use no parentheses.* Newspaper articles (see our footnote 5, above) follow the same pattern. With a book, a popular magazine, or a newspaper you use "p." before the page number; with a magazine having a Roman volume number, do not use "p.": "XXIX (1919), 23-26." Give the second page number in full: "23-26" not "23-6." A book's year is the year of copyright, usually given on the back of the title page. The point of footnoting, of course, is to identify author, title, publication, and page, to exhibit your sources fully to the reader, who might want to use them himself. Here are some complications:

¹ Abraham B. Caldwell, "The Case for Subsidized Television," *American Questioner*, June 20, 1957, p. 37, quoted Albert N. Mendenhall, *The Time Is Now* (Princeton, 1962), p. 308.

[You have found the quotation in Mendenhall's book.]

¹ D. C. Hill, "Who Is Communicating What?" in *Essays for Study*, ed. James L. McDonald and Leonard P. Doan (New York, 1959), p. 214, reprinted from *Era*, XII (1955).

[McDonald and Doan have edited the collection. You could have cited *Era* first, and given pages for both. A title ending in a question mark should not take a comma.]

¹ Arnold Peters, "Medicine," *Encyc. Brit.*, 14th ed. (Chicago, 1952).

[Abbreviate familiar titles, so long as they remain clear. You need neither volume nor page numbers in alphabetized encyclopedias. Here the article was initialed "A.P.," and you have looked up the author's name at the front of the volume.]

¹ "Prunes," *Encyc. Brit.*, 14th ed. (Chicago, 1952).

[Here the article was not initialed.]

¹ George L. Gillies, "Robert Herrick's 'Corinna'," *House and Home*, II (1881), 490.

[This shows where to put the comma when the title of a magazine article ends in a quotation, and you have to use both single and double quotation marks. Gillies's original title would have looked like this: Robert Herrick's "Corinna."]

¹ *The Merchant of Venice* I.ii.102, in *The Complete Works of Shakespeare*, ed. George Lyman Kittredge (Boston, 1936).

[Note the absence of the comma after the title, and the periods and close spacing between Act.scene.line. Subsequent references would go directly in your text within parentheses: (*Merch.* IV.iii.11–12). See further instructions below.]

These should cover most footnoting problems, or suggest how to meet them.

Abbreviate your references after the first full citation. Two old favorite abbreviations are now mercifully out of style. Do NOT use:

ibid.—*ibidem* ("in the same place"), meaning the title cited in the note directly before. Instead, use the author's last name, and give the page.

op. cit.—*opera citato* ("in the work cited"), meaning title referred to again after other notes have intervened. Again, use the author's last name instead, and give the page.

Four are still used and useful (do *not* italicize them):

cf.—*confer* (means "compare"); do not use it for "see."

et al.—*et alii* ("and others"); does not mean "and all"; use it after the first author in multiple authorships, "Ronald Elkins et al."

loc. cit.—*loco citato* ("in the place cited"); use without page number, when you cite a page previously noted. Best in parentheses *in the text:* "Allenberg (loc. cit.) also considers this important."

passim—(not an abbreviation; a Latin word meaning "throughout the work; here and there"). Use when a writer makes the same point in many places within a single work; use also for statistics you have compiled from observations and tables scattered throughout his work.

Our footnotes to the television paper might continue like this, with abbreviations for works already fully cited:

[6] Allenberg, p. 12.

[7] Allenberg, p. 13.

[Would have been "Ibid., p. 13," but the name is clearer.]

[8] Jones, passim.

[9] Allenberg, p. 4.

[Would have been "Allenberg, op. cit., p. 4."]

[10] Cf. Dillon et al., p. 191—exactly the opposite position.

[11] See Jones, p. 24, for a reasonable and full denial of this claim.

[12] See Weiss, p. 6, and Smith, p. 71.

[13] Jones, loc. cit.; cf. Weiss, p. 3.

["Loc. cit." means the last Jones citation—p. 24—to which we are asking our readers to compare Weiss's position, indicating simply that Weiss is a little extreme.]

If we had two Joneses, our short references would simply have had to repeat first initials; if Jones had written two articles or books, we would have picked two convenient but clear short titles for subsequent references. In addition to Jones's article, "Television and Vision: The Case for Governmental Control," suppose we have also cited his book, *The Kinescopic Arts and Sciences* (Princeton, 1950). Our further references to him would look like this:

⁴ Jones, "Vision," p. 27.

⁵ Jones, *Kinescopic Arts*, p. 291.

Abbreviate books of the Bible, even the first time. The Bible and its books, though capitalized as ordinary titles, are never italicized. Biblical references go directly into your text, within parentheses—no footnote, no commas, *small* Roman numerals for chapter, Arabic for verse: Mark xvi.6; Jer. vi.24; II Sam. xviii.33. No comma—only a space—separates name from numbers; periods separate the numbers, *with no spacing*. The dictionary gives the accepted abbreviations: Gen., Exod., Lev., Deut. Make Biblical references like this:

> There is still nothing new under the sun (Eccl. i.9); man still does not live by bread alone (Matt. iv.4).
> As Ecclesiastes tells us, "there is no new thing under the sun" (i.9).

Abbreviate plays and long poems after the first time. Handle plays and long poems like Biblical citations, after an initial footnote identifying the edition (see page 128). Italicize the title: *Romeo* II.iv.72–75 [this is *Romeo and Juliet*, Act II, Scene iv, lines 72–75]; *Caesar* V.iii.6; *Ham.* I.i.23; *Iliad* IX.93; *P.L.* IV.918 [*Paradise Lost*, Book IV, line 918]. Use the numbers alone if you have already mentioned the title, or have clearly implied it, as in repeated quotations from the same work.

Match your bibliography to your footnotes. When your paper is finally typed, alphabetize the cards of the works cited in your footnotes (by authors' last names or, with anonymous works, by first words of titles—not counting, but keeping, *The, A,* or *An*). You will not have used all your notes, nor all the articles you have carded. Pass over them in decent silence. *Include no work not specifically cited.* Your bibliographical entries will be just like your footnotes except that: (1) you will put the author's last name first;

(2) you will give the total span of pages for magazine articles—none at all for books; (3) you will reverse indentation so that the author's name will stand out; (4) you will punctuate differently—putting one period after the alphabetized name or title, and another (no parenthesis) after a *book's* place and date of publication; and (5) you will double-space, triple-spacing between entries. Your single-spacing has been the typewriter's approximation of passages set in small print. If you had been actually writing for print, you would have double-spaced everything and would not have put your footnotes at the bottoms of pages: you would have collected them serially at the end of the paper in a section headed "Footnotes." In many publications you would not have a bibliography; in many others, you would. Your research paper requires one, something like this:

BIBLIOGRAPHY

Allenberg, Donald. *The Future of Television.* New York, 1958.

Brown, J. P. "Some Facts About Television and Education," *New Mercury,* July 10, 1958, pp. 20–31.

Cummings, John L. "How Good Are Our Programs?" *Time and Tide,* XLVI (1962), 163–176.

The Encyclopaedia Britannica. 14th ed. 24 vols. Chicago, 1952.

Jones, Bingham. *The Kinescopic Arts and Sciences.* Princeton, 1950.

———. "Television and Vision: The Case for Governmental Control," *Independent Review,* VII (1959), 18–31.

"The Trouble with Television." Anon. editorial, New York *Times,* April 10, 1961, Sec. 4, p. 8.

[Each new section of this paper begins its numbering anew; hence, "Sec. 4." Notice that the city, which practically forms a part of the title, is nevertheless NOT italicized with newspapers: New York *Herald Tribune,* Detroit *Free Press.*]

I have based these instructions on *The MLA Style Sheet* (compiled by the Modern Language Association of America), which you may consult for further detail. It is standard for work in literature and the humanities. The sciences use slightly different conventions. Bingham Jones's article would look like this in a botanical bibliography (no italics, no quotation marks, no parentheses)—

old hat.) Government television control should be   *Wordy*

exercised by a committee of prominent citizens and

awk   people interested in entertainment-type programs

appointed by the president. The people are interested

in T. V., and the people should be given a voice. By ?

the use of A committee T. V. could be fairly and

effectively controlled. This would be Modern. *transition*

DM —Returning to finances, the companies could still place

their advertisements between shows, but they would not

control the shows. Advertising and showmanship would

be kept seperate. It would still sell soap and *sp.*

cigarettes and everything the public demands and maybe

make a contribution toward making this a better world — *trite*

in which to live, for not only the people but for the // st

advertisers too.

Sensible control would be both democratic and // st

help improve the intellectual level.

C — Idea good, plan good, research good — and your
argument is persuasive. You still can catch an
apt phrase now and then, BUT (!) you've fallen into
all your old habits in the push. Avoid clusters of nouns
like government television control — 3 in a row! Avoid
the passive voice and all the excess wordage. The
end seems lame. And please learn to punctuate. This
deserves rewriting. Spend some time on it, sentence
by sentence. I'll be happy to reconsider the grade.

old hat." The government should control television only
through a committee of prominent citizens appointed by
the President. For balance, the committee should
include a few champions of light entertainment. Since,
in a sense, television is really public property, the
public should have some voice in television's affairs.
After all, representative government is the modern way.

Nor would business go unrepresented. Business
would still manage its own house, and it would have
seats on the governmental committee. Companies could
still bid for advertising space between the best programs,
but they could no longer influence the programs themselves.
Advertising would exercise its showmanship only in
advertising. It would still sell its soap and cigarettes,
but the programs themselves would be freed for variety
and creativity. New audiences might even benefit the
advertisers, and sensible control of the commercial
motive would certainly increase everyone's opportunity
to see for himself.

B+ Nice work! I like "champions of light entertainment"
and "see for himself." This is the style you've been
working for: not too big, not too little, sensible, clear,
on its toes. You are touching the concrete beautifully:
house, seats, soap and cigarettes.
    Since this is a second chance, I can't give highest
honors. But its a fine job. Congratulations. You're
really writing in Style ____!

Television and Vision: The Case for Governmental Control. Independent Review. 8:18–31. For some advanced courses you may want to consult:

> *Publication Manual of the American Psychological Association.* Washington, D.C., 1957.
> *Style Manual.* U.S. Government Printing Office. Rev. ed. Washington, D.C., 1959.
> *Style Manual for Biological Journals.* Washington, D.C., 1960.
> Wood, George McLane. *Suggestions to Authors . . . , United States Geological Survey.* 4th ed. rev. by Bernard H. Lane. Washington, D.C., 1935.

But for the present, let us suppose that you have finally turned your paper in. After all that researching, carding, plotting, revising, and typing, you are now dismayed as your instructor hands back your paper thoroughly penciled (with marks much like those inside the back cover of this book). Pages 132 and 133 give a sample of your trouble and of your final corrections. They should also demonstrate the value of a good antagonistic friend in helping you check the common tendency to become hypnotized by your own writing, to stand convinced that your words say what you intended, when in fact they may say other things to other people. You will perhaps have had the foresight to plan and revise your writing against the Check List inside the front cover before submitting your paper in final form. If so, you will doubtless have saved such a friend some trouble. You may even win his praise!

SUGGESTED TOPICS

T.W.A. Power
Socialized Medicine
Euthanasia
Capital Punishment
Early Reviews of *For Whom the Bell Tolls*
Robert Taft's Foreign Policy

Light and Dark in Three Poems by Robert Frost
Interracial Marriage
Suffrage at Eighteen
Censorship
States' Rights
Federal Aid to Education

Index